ACCOUNTING *for* SMALL BUSINESS OWNERS

Workforce Development Collection

**Funded by
The California State Library
Initiatives Book Project**

RIVERSIDE
PUBLIC LIBRARY

ACCOUNTING
for SMALL BUSINESS OWNERS

TYCHO
PRESS

CONTENTS

INTRODUCTION

Accounting is a large and multifaceted field that encompasses many business activities. It serves a fundamental role in businesses of all types, from multinational corporations to nationwide chains to mom-and-pop neighborhood stores. In this book we're going to break it all down at the level of the small business owner. We'll discuss what accounting is and the industry rules that govern how accountants operate. You'll learn about financial statements—what they are and how to use them. We'll cover stock, payroll, borrowing, and employee benefit and tax payments. Then we'll go over production and inventory, as well as paying bills and expenses.

After reading this book you should have an understanding of some basic principles of accounting and be able to set up your first set of books for your small business. You'll be able to prepare your own financial statements and determine whether or not your business is making a profit. You'll also be able to better predict the ups and downs of your business and make more informed decisions, which will keep your enterprise healthy and growing.

WHAT IS ACCOUNTING?

Accounting is the process of recording business transactions, summarizing that data in financial statements, analyzing it, and then reporting the findings to owners and investors. Owners of small businesses need to know if their sales, costs, and expenses are increasing or decreasing, and if they are making a profit or a loss during a specified time period. A business owner can't improve the business unless they know what is and isn't working.

As a small business owner, you will need to monitor cash flow so you'll know if you have enough to cover your upcoming expenses. You'll also need to keep an eye on receivables and payables so you know if customers are paying you on time, and that you're paying your vendors timely as well. You'll need to monitor your sales and expenses to make sure you are earning a profit. If you're losing money, there's not much point to being in business!

WHO GOVERNS THE ACCOUNTING INDUSTRY?

The Federal Accounting Standards Board (FASB) is the governing body that establishes and issues the standards to which all certified public accountants (CPAs) must adhere. FASB standards, known as generally accepted accounting principles (GAAP—pronounced "gap"), consist of a set of guidelines that govern how the accounting industry performs its duties. The goal is to ensure credibility and transparency within the industry.

The basic accounting principles include:

- **Cost principle**. Accountants use the term *cost* for the amount originally spent, so amounts shown on financial statements are referred to as "historical costs."
- **Economic entity assumption principle**. Accountants consider the business and its owner as separate entities.
- **Full disclosure principle**. If certain information would be relevant to an investor or lender, it should be disclosed in the financial statements. The information is usually included in the form of footnotes.
- **Going concern principle**. Accountants act on the assumption that the business will keep operating indefinitely.
- **Matching principle**. Accountants try to match revenue to expenses (i.e., post them in the time period, month, or quarter in which they were earned). This principle is used in the accrual method of accounting.
- **Revenue recognition principle**. Accountants recognize revenue as it is earned, not as cash is received. This system is also used in the accrual method.

A few of these principles are specific only to the accrual method of accounting, as opposed to the cash method. The accrual method recognizes revenue when it is earned (when the product is shipped or services are performed) and expenses when they are incurred (purchases made), not necessarily when money is exchanged. This method allows the business owner to keep the revenue and expenses for products sold or services performed reported in the same time period, such as over a 30-day period.

That said, most small businesses use the cash method, which is acknowledged by governing agencies as an acceptable alternative. This method stipulates that revenue be recognized when the cash is received and that expenses be posted when the bill is paid.

BOOKKEEPERS, ACCOUNTANTS, CONTROLLERS, AND CPAS: WHO DOES WHAT?

Accounting personnel have many job titles, and each specializes in different tasks and duties. If you ever need to hire someone to help you with accounting, you will need to know how these titles differ.

A bookkeeper posts transactions and "keeps the books" by recording customer payments and bill payments. This job entails invoicing customers, paying bills, paying employees, making deposits, and so on.

An accountant picks up where the bookkeeper leaves off. An accountant takes the information the bookkeeper records and summarizes that information into financial statements. Accountants also conduct a financial analysis on the data in those statements to determine the financial health of the company.

A controller (or comptroller) is a job designation found in larger organizations. This person serves as the "head accountant" for the company, usually overseeing a department of several accountants or bookkeepers. This person may report to the owner directly; in larger corporations he or she would report to the treasurer or VP of Finance. The controller keeps the accounting processes on track by making sure all duties are performed accurately and timely, and works with the company owners to help fulfill the business's financial objectives.

A CPA is an accountant who has passed a test (the Uniform CPA Examination) to perform higher-level accounting work, somewhat like an attorney passes the bar exam before practicing law. A CPA may then prepare reviewed or audited financial statements for companies and represent businesses before the IRS in tax matters. During an audit, the CPA goes into a business and examines the accounting records, pulls samples, and tests for the accuracy of financial statements. The CPA can then give an opinion on the accuracy of those records and on whether there are any pending issues that may affect the statements.

An accountant who is not a CPA may only prepare compiled financial statements. These statements are nonreviewed—meaning they're prepared specifically from the business owner's data—and the accountant may not give an opinion on the statements.

The accounting work required by every small business will vary according to the needs of the owner and the legal structure of the business. An owner should be familiar with the basics of the five main business structures because his or her company will have to be registered as one of them: A business can be structured as a sole proprietorship, a partnership, an LLC, an S corporation, or a C corporation. Let's look at these in more detail.

BUSINESS STRUCTURES

An experienced attorney will be able to help you decide which legal structure is right for you and your business.

Sole Proprietorship

A sole proprietorship is the simplest business structure. The business is run as an extension of the owner. Essentially, the owner *is* the business. Most part-time and very small businesses follow this model. Business activity is reported on IRS Form 1040, using Schedule C. The owner of a sole proprietorship calculates and pays self-employment taxes on Schedule SE, with the Form 1040. Any legal debts of the business are the owner's personally.

Partnership

A partnership is like a sole proprietorship, only there is more than one owner. There may be two owners or twenty. Each partner is proportionately responsible for business debts, and each shares in any profits or losses. The partnership is an entity and as such files a Form 1065 Partnership Tax Return. Each owner receives a Form K-1 and reports the business activity on his or her personal tax return.

LLC

A limited liability company (LLC) is a designation given by the IRS and is popular because it helps protect the small business owner from the legal liabilities of the business. An LLC can be operated as a partnership or as an S corporation—the business owner chooses when the company is formed. This requires the services of an attorney. An LLC files its own tax return, either as a Form 1065 for an LLC treated as a partnership, or as a Form 1120-S if the LLC is treated as an S corporation.

S Corporation

Being designated as a S corporation is also a popular choice for small business owners because it affords the protection of a corporation without the separate taxation issues (a regular corporation is required to file a tax return, IRS Form 1120, and pays taxes on the profits). An S corporation files a Form 1065 Partnership Tax Return, and the owners—even if there is only one—get a Form K-1 and report all business profits or losses on their personal tax returns. One issue to be aware of here is that the IRS has been targeting S corporations for payroll avoidance. If you do operate as an S corporation, you will need to pay yourself as an employee for at least "reasonable" compensation and pay payroll taxes on those wages.

C Corporation

A C corporation is its own entity and affords the owners personal protection from any legal liabilities. However, a C corporation is required to pay taxes on profits, and the corporate tax rate may be higher than an owner's personal tax rate. Also, the owners of a C corporation will have to pay taxes on their payroll and dividends personally.

TYPES OF SMALL BUSINESSES

Although small businesses are as unique as the owners who start them, most will fall into one of three main industry categories:

- Manufacturing
- Wholesale/Retail
- Service

The main differentiator is whether the business sells goods or services, which determines its accounting systems and methods. A business will do one of the following: produce goods for sale (manufacturer), provide services for sale (service provider), or buy products to resell (wholesaler/retailer).

The manufacturer buys materials and produces a product, which it then sells, either to other businesses or to consumers. A manufacturer will need to account for the cost of goods sold (materials purchased, labor costs, freight) and inventory (materials to be used, product waiting to be sold).

The service business provides a service—be it landscaping or insurance, computer repair or wedding planning—to other businesses or to consumers. A service provider won't have any inventory, but instead will have cost of sales (presentation costs, travel costs, equipment).

The wholesale business buys products and sells them to retailers for what's called a markup. That means the wholesaler adds a certain percentage to the price to cover its costs and make a profit. The retailer buys that product and then sells the product to consumers for a little more than it bought the product for—to cover its costs and make a profit. These businesses will have a cost of goods sold (product purchased) and will have to account for the inventory of those products.

HELPFUL HINTS (for all kinds of businesses)

- Use a separate checking account for your business.

- Get and use a federal Taxpayer Identification Number (TIN). This saves you from having to use your Social Security Number for identification.

- Don't use your personal credit card for business expenses; Get a separate business card.

- Keep track of all cash received from sales or incidentals for your business, and hold on to invoices.

- Keep track of all cash spent for business use, and store receipts for everything.

- Designate a file drawer or box for your business files, and use it to keep all legal agreements and documents well organized and accessible.

- If you buy any assets—equipment, vehicles, investments, furniture—keep all receipts in a separate file. You will need to report them to your accountant for depreciation.

- Keep track of any money or equipment that you personally contribute to the business. You need a record to help you verify the cost of that contribution.

- Don't pay personal bills out of the business checking account. If you do, it will have to be posted as an owner withdrawal.

So far we've discussed what accounting is, the rules that govern the industry, and some of the job titles you may encounter. We've also gone over the different types of business and some of their issues, as well as tips to keep in mind as you start your own business.

As a small business owner, you can do your own accounting, or you may want to hire someone. Whatever you choose, you'll still need to understand the accounting process, your books, and what they tell you about your business. The rest of this book will show you how.

BASIC ACCOUNTING TERMS

You will be hearing (and using) certain accounting terms, concepts, and processes repeatedly, so you'll want to have a solid understanding of them. For example, you'll need to know how to categorize your assets, expenses, and liabilities, which will mean creating a list of accounts. You'll want to learn how to create financial statements such as income statements and balance sheets, and how to interpret them to find ways to improve your business. These are all building blocks of accounting. But underlying all of them is one of the most important concepts to accounting systems and methods: the accounting equation.

THE ACCOUNTING EQUATION

The accounting equation is a fundamental principle of accounting. It represents the relationship between three components of your business:

ASSETS (What You Own)
LIABILITIES (What You Owe)
EQUITY (The Difference between Your Assets and Liabilities)

The accounting equation is written as follows:

ASSETS = LIABILITIES + EQUITY

If your books are done correctly, the two sides of this equation will always equal each other. Accounting is a double-entry system, meaning that for every transaction that affects one side of the equation, there is a corresponding change (of equal amount) on the other side.

Let's say you bring in a printer from home for your business to use. According to the logic of the double-entry system, two things just happened: Your company gained a piece of equipment (thereby increasing assets by, say, $200), and equity increased by that same $200. In other words, the increase is accounted for on both sides of the equation.

Accountants refer to these business transactions as debits and credits. All our transactions are either debits or credits: For every debit there is a credit. Debits are the left side of the equation, and credits are the right side. Debits increase asset accounts. Credits increase liabilities and equity accounts. We'll go deeper into this in chapter 2.

A final note on the accounting equation: when we are discussing sole proprietorships, equity is "owner's equity." It belongs to the business owner. When we are looking at corporations, equity is "stockholders' equity." It is shared by the stockholders.

What Is a Chart of Accounts?

A chart of accounts is simply a list of all the accounts you will be using in your bookkeeping. *Account* is an accounting term used to describe a certain classification of a transaction. Don't think of it like a checking account—think of it as a box. In each box, you will keep all like transactions. For example, all sales go into a box (account), and all office supply purchases go into a box (account). Your accounts will be divided into the following categories: assets, liabilities, equity, revenue, and expenses (see figure 1).

Your chart of accounts will determine how you record your business transactions and is the basis of all your important financial statements. Your accounts always tie back to the larger principle of the accounting equation—they are simply subcategories of the components of the equation.

If you've ever seen a balance sheet, you'll notice that it is set up like the accounting equation (see table 1). Assets, liabilities, and equity are all separated into different sections. If you compare the total amounts, you'll see that total assets equals total liabilities plus equity, just as in the equation.

CHART OF ACCOUNTS

ASSETS	Cash Accounts Receivable Inventory Investments Property & Equipment Accumulated Depreciation
LIABILITIES	Accounts Payable Credit Card Payable Notes Payable
EQUITY	Owners Equity (or Retained Earnings for a corporation)
REVENUE	Sales Returns Miscellaneous Income Interest Income
EXPENSES	Wages Payroll Taxes Employee Benefits Rent Utilities Advertising Insurance Professional Fees

Figure 1. Chart of Accounts

XYZ CLEANERS BALANCE SHEET AS OF JULY 31 2020		
ASSETS:		
CHECKING ACCOUNT	$5,750	
ACCOUNTS RECEIVABLE	$3,500	
TOTAL ASSETS		$9,250
LIABILITIES:		
CREDIT CARD PAYABLE	$950	
PAYROLL TAXES PAYABLE	$1,300	
TOTAL LIABILITIES	$2,250	
EQUITY:		
OWNER'S EQUITY	$7,000	
TOTAL LIAB. & EQUITY		$9,250

Table 1. Sample balance sheet

At the end of every month (or quarter or year), an accounting procedure is done that closes out all revenue and expense accounts into the owner's equity account.

At the beginning of each year you will start over at zero with revenue and expenses. The profit or loss from the previous year will be reflected in the equity accounts—either owner's equity or stockholders' equity (recorded as retained earnings for corporations). Essentially, this means that the profit or loss for that time period will be posted into the owner's equity account. A profit will increase equity, and a loss will decrease it. Put another way, an increase in a revenue account will increase equity, and an increase in an expense account will decrease it.

When thinking about equity, always remember that "what you own, less what you owe, is the net worth of your business."

THE BALANCE SHEET

The balance sheet is one of the primary financial statements used by business owners and accountants. It gives you a snapshot of your business at a specific date. As we'll see later, other statements report numbers for periods of time (a month, a quarter, a year), but a balance sheet reflects the company's financial standing at that instant. It is useful to investors, bankers, and owners who want a quick financial snapshot of the business.

The balance sheet lists your assets (what you own), your liabilities (what you owe), and your equity (what's left). The "what's left" part is the health of your business—it's what your investment in the business is worth (as shown in the equity section). Your owner's equity (or retained earnings in a corporation) shows you the accumulated earnings of the company.

If you had to liquidate your business tomorrow, you'd sell your assets to pay your liabilities. The equity you have in your business is what you would walk away with.

You can also use your balance sheet to see your cash balance, how much your customers owe you (accounts receivable), and how much you owe your vendors (accounts payable). You'll see any long-term debt (loans) in the liability section. If you watch your balance sheet from year to year, you will see whether you're accumulating more cash or more debt.

Let's look more closely at the components of the balance sheet.

Assets

Assets are the things you own, such as cash, receivables (money customers owe you), inventory, investments, cars, trucks, furniture, computers, buildings, and so on.

Assets are listed in a certain way, starting with what we call current assets, which are highly liquid and can easily be turned into cash.

Next you have long-term assets. One kind of long-term asset is plant assets (*plant* refers to a business location and includes buildings, equipment, furniture, etc.). Long-term assets, such as buildings and equipment, take longer to be turned into cash and are intended to be kept long-term.

Another kind of long-term asset is intangible assets, such as patents, trademarks, and goodwill. These stay on the balance sheet forever.

If you see *goodwill* on a balance sheet, you'll know the business, or at least part of it, was purchased from another owner. Goodwill represents the excess of the purchase price over the fair market value of the assets purchased.

Say a business has assets equal to $100,000, but someone is willing to pay $125,000 for it. The extra amount is labeled goodwill and represents the loyal customers and the reputation in the community, which the new owner hopes to keep. Basically, it's the value of the company's brand.

Another long-term asset you may see on a balance sheet is a customer list. Service-dominated businesses, such as insurance companies, would list this asset. It represents the loyal customers (which are really the core value of the business) that the agency is "selling" to the new owner. This asset is amortized (paid off, like depreciation) over 15 years.

Liabilities

Liabilities are things you owe, such as utility bills or materials purchased. These are called accounts payable, things you've purchased "on time" (i.e., you get a bill in the mail and pay it within 10 or 30 days).

Liabilities are also listed as current and long-term, with current liabilities listed first. Current liabilities are bills that are payable within one year. These include accounts payable, credit card payable, payroll taxes payable, lines of credit payable, and so forth. Long-term liabilities are things you owe that will take more than one year to pay, such as mortgages, car loans, large bank loans, and owner loans to the company.

Large firms show the "current portion of long-term debt" in their current liabilities section. This shows one year of payments on their long-term debt that will be paid off within one year. It's deducted from the long-term portion at the beginning of the year.

Equity

Equity is sometimes called capital or net worth. For a sole proprietor, equity is the amount of owner contributions less owner withdrawals, plus profit (or minus loss). The balance sheet equity section will show the account as owner capital. This account includes all owner contributions to the company, withdrawals from the company, and all profits and/or losses.

For a partnership, multiple owner accounts will be listed.

For a corporation, you will see the accounts common stock (the stock issued by the corporation), retained earnings, undistributed earnings, dividends, and maybe treasury stock. You may also see preferred stock, depending on the type of stock issued.

Retained earnings is the accumulation of previous profits and losses. Undistributed earnings is the current year's profit or loss, which until your year-end close is "undistributed." In the year-end close process, all income and expense accounts are closed into your retained earnings account.

Treasury stock represents any stock the corporation has bought back.

Let's look at an example of how it all fits together. Table 2 shows the balance sheet for XYZ Cleaners. It's a sole proprietorship, meaning the owner is not incorporated and there are no partners. It sells cleaning services rather than manufactured goods.

Notice the heading. It says "as of July 31, 2020." This report is showing the financial snapshot of this company as of July 31.

XYZ CLEANERS BALANCE SHEET AS OF JULY 31, 2020		
ASSETS:		
CHECKING ACCOUNT	$5,750	
ACCOUNTS RECEIVABLE	$3,500	
TOTAL ASSETS		$9,250
LIABILITIES:		
CREDIT CARD PAYABLE	$950	
PAYROLL TAXES PAYABLE	$1,300	
TOTAL LIABILITIES	$2,250	
EQUITY:		
OWNER'S EQUITY	$7,000	
TOTAL LIAB. & EQUITY		$9,250

Table 2. Balance sheet for XYZ Cleaners

Assets

In this very simple balance sheet, there is no distinction made between current and long-term assets, since this small business owner didn't have much to list.

As mentioned above, assets are always listed in order of what can be called "cash-ability." Accounting textbooks talk about liquidity, which is the same idea, but both seek to answer the question, How easily is the asset turned into cash?

Obviously, any checking or savings account will be listed first, since those *are* cash. In the case of XYZ, that is what we see listed first under assets.

Next we see accounts receivable, which is fairly easily turned into cash— just get your customers to pay you.

You wouldn't think a small cleaner would have receivables, but he may have a business laundry account, and customers pay him 10 or 30 days after he bills them. If all those customers settled their bills today, the owner would have $9,250 total in cash.

In our example, this cleaner rents a store and is not listing any equipment, so maybe he's renting a space that's already furnished.

Liabilities

The owner has a credit card payable account listed, so we can assume that he pays for supplies on a credit card. He also has payroll taxes, which would be federal, state, and local withholding taxes due. If he owned a larger organization, he might also show unemployment and workers compensation taxes due.

This is also where you would see accounts payable and any loans.

Equity

There is only one owner in this example, so you just see his owner's equity account, which includes any of his personal contributions to the business, any withdrawals he's taken out of the business, and all of his profits and/or losses.

Remember that Assets = Liabilities + Equity. This will *always* be the case, and takes us back to the fundamental accounting equation. What you own, less what you owe, is your net worth (equity) in the business.

Every business owner should watch her balance sheet each month to see if the business is growing. If not, she has the opportunity to correct the situation as soon as she becomes aware of it. If she waits until year-end, it may be too late to boost a depressed bottom line.

Let's move on to a slightly more involved balance sheet example. Table 3 shows the balance sheet for Mountain Man Outfitters, Inc., a corporation with one owner. The store has three locations (which we see broken out in the income statement section), but for the purposes of the balance sheet, this owner has chosen to consolidate all locations into one statement to get a comprehensive view of the company's financial picture.

Notice the heading, "as of Dec 31, 2020," which tells you that this is a year-end balance sheet. Accountants like to analyze company financial information as "year-ends," but you can prepare a balance sheet for any day, at any time.

Assets

Unlike XYZ, Mountain Man Outfitters has both current and long-term assets. Long-term assets are also called "fixed assets" or "plant assets" (as they are here).

Current Assets

Again, these are listed in order of cash-ability. Cash comes first, closely followed by savings and investments, which in this case means certificates of deposit or money market accounts—not investments in companies. If you do have an investment in a company, that would be listed under long-term assets.

Next come accounts receivable and inventory. The latter would be product on the sales floor or in storage. Then we have the value of securities, which are stocks and/or bonds. The balance in your investment accounts is usually the current value as of the last year-end, which is when accountants generally update balances.

This business has a lot of cash and savings. It also has a relatively large amount of receivables.

Long-Term Assets

As we'll see in Mountain Man's income statement, one of the three locations owns a building, and all three have furniture and computer equipment owned by the company. So all of the equipment and furniture, plus the one building, make up the long-term assets.

Here, we have plant assets and no intangibles. There is no goodwill, so we know this business was not purchased. Notice the plant assets are listed with the corresponding accumulated depreciation (more on that later), and with a net value carried over into the next column. So we can see, at a glance, the approximate net value (also called "book value") of each asset. For example, the furniture was purchased for $230,000, but is now worth roughly $115,000.

MOUNTAIN MAN OUTFITTERS, INC.
BALANCE SHEET AS OF DECEMBER 31, 2020

ASSETS:			
CURRENT ASSETS:			
CASH		$165,000	
SAVINGS		$250,000	
ACCOUNTS RECEIVABLE		$115,000	
INVENTORY		$750,000	
INVESTMENT IN SECURITIES		$320,000	
TOTAL CURRENT ASSETS			**$1,600,000**
PLANT ASSETS:			
FURNITURE & FIXTURES	$230,000		
LESS ACCUMULATED DEPRECIATION	$-115,000	$115,000	
COMPUTER EQUIPMENT	$90,000		
LESS ACCUMULATED DEPRECIATION	$-35,000	$55,000	
BUILDING & IMPROVEMENTS	$420,000		
LESS ACCUMULATED DEPRECIATION	$-80,000	$340,000	
TOTAL PLANT ASSETS			**$510,000**
TOTAL ASSETS			**$2,110,000**
LIABILITIES:			
CURRENT LIABILITIES:			
ACCOUNTS PAYABLE	$115,000		
PAYROLL TAXES PAYABLE	$43,000		
SALES TAX PAYABLE	$52,000		
TOTAL CURRENT LIABILITIES		**$210,000**	
LONG-TERM LIABILITIES:			
NOTE PAYABLE–OWNER	$150,000		
NOTE PAYABLE–PNC BANK	$95,000		
NOTE PAYABLE–MORTGAGE	$365,000		
TOTAL LONG-TERM LIABILITIES		**$610,000**	
TOTAL LIABILITIES			**$820,000**
EQUITY:			
COMMON STOCK		$1,000	
RETAINED EARNINGS		$839,000	
UNDISTRIBUTED EARNINGS		$650,000	
DIVIDENDS		$-200,000	
TOTAL EQUITY			**$1,290,000**
TOTAL LIABILITIES & EQUITY			**$2,110,000**

Table 3. Balance sheet for Mountain Man Outfitters, Inc.

We know this business has $1,600,000 in current assets, which can be readily turned into cash. And it has $510,000 in long-term assets (plant assets), which are more of a long-term investment for the company. This gives the company $2,110,000 in total assets.

This is the first half of the balance sheet.

The second half contains the liabilities and equity. And, remember, each half will match: ASSETS = LIABILITIES + EQUITY.

Liabilities

Just as it was with the assets, a distinction has been made here between current and long-term liabilities.

Current liabilities for this business are accounts payable (corporate accounts that pay in 30 days as opposed to regular retail shoppers, who pay at purchase), payroll taxes payable (employer's Social Security and Medicare taxes, unemployment taxes, and workers' compensation taxes), and sales tax payable (sales taxes due on retail sales). The company's current liabilities total $210,000.

This represents items that need to be paid within a short time, perhaps within a month or a quarter, but definitely within a year.

Anything due within a longer time period is considered a long-term liability.

Long-Term Liabilities

The long-term liabilities here include a mortgage on the owned building, a note payable–owner, and another bank loan.

The note payable–owner reflects money the owner has put into the business. If this were a sole proprietorship, it would be called a capital contribution and would be in the equity section. But since this is a corporation, in which the business is

QUICK TIP Use the debt-to-asset ratio to compare your net plant assets to your loans payable (leave out the owner loan). In table 3 we see net plant assets of $510,000 and loans of $95,000 and $365,000, for a total of $460,000. This shows that the asset value is more than the loan value, meaning (one hopes) that you can sell the assets and pay off the loans if necessary.

an entity separate from the owner, a loan document called a note payable has been prepared instead.

The current and long-term liabilities amounts are totaled, giving a total liabilities amount of $820,000.

Equity

Whether it's an S or C corporation, equity accounts include common stock and retained earnings.

In this example, the company has common stock of $1,000, which is probably just the one owner's stock. It also has retained earnings of $839,000, which is the accumulated profits and losses for the history of the company.

The company also shows undistributed earnings of $650,000, which is the current year's profit. It's called "undistributed" because it has not yet been distributed to stockholders in the way of dividends. After dividends have been paid out, the balance will be moved to retained earnings.

Now we see another account called dividends. When an owner of a corporation takes profits out of the company, it is called dividends and is subtracted from the other equity accounts. In this example, the owner took out $200,000. He could have had a significant personal need, bought a large asset, or made an investment that he wanted to own personally rather than through the company.

Now the equity accounts are combined, and then the total liabilities and total equity amounts are added together. This amount matches total assets.

AGAIN: ASSETS = LIABILITIES + EQUITY.

The balance sheet shows you the health of your business. Are you bringing cash into the organization? Are your assets more than your liabilities? In other words, do you own more than you owe? If the answer is no, you have a weak organization.

But you won't know that unless you stay abreast of your balance sheet.

Let's move on to our next financial statement—the income statement.

THE INCOME STATEMENT

The income statement, another vital financial statement, has a different purpose than a balance sheet. It tells you how your business performed during a range of time, not in a particular moment. It shows you what happened with your sales, cost of sales, expenses, and profit or loss over time.

The income statement is also called a profit and loss statement because after subtracting expenses from revenue, you will have either a profit or a loss. While that's essential to know, there's also a wealth of other information hidden in this statement.

The income statement is set up in a very specific way. The heading will say something like "for the month of" or "for the year ended." The range of time you designate for the statement may be a month, a quarter, a year, or whatever duration you prefer.

The format of an income statement is specific, too.

Revenue (sales) is listed first, then, if applicable, cost of goods sold for manufacturers and cost of sales for retailers, then gross margin (also called operating profit), then expenses, then finally profit or loss. Let's look at these in turn.

Revenue

Revenue is also referred to as sales, although you may have a revenue item that is not sales, such as interest income or scrap income (*scrap income* is leftover from manufacturing that is then sold to someone who recycles or repurposes it—like steel). You may see revenue listed as just one line item or as several lines separating sales by location, by product, or by whatever distinction you want to make. You will be able to compare sales on your income statements each month so you can use the categories to track your sales however you want. You will want to have a separate revenue account for each of these income streams (such as interest income or scrap income). Any money coming into your business is either income or a loan.

Cost of Goods Sold (COGS) or Cost of Sales (COS)

COGS is the term used for manufacturers, and COS is used for retailers or service providers. The purpose of this section is to list the direct costs of making or selling the products or of offering the service for sale. These would include the cost of materials for manufacture or products for resale, the cost of labor directly related to the manufacture or sale, freight to get the product to market, and subcontracted services used.

Gross Margin

Gross margin is also called operating profit. It is the amount of money left over after you deduct your cost of goods sold from your total revenue, which is used to cover the other costs of doing business (e.g., rent, utilities, administrative wages, advertising). Gross margin tells you, in a general sense, whether you made money from your products or service.

Expenses

Expenses, also called operating expenses, are your general costs of doing business. Whether or not you make a sale, you have to pay the rent and utilities. You may also need to pay for advertising, legal/accounting advice, computers, subscriptions/dues, bank fees, repairs and maintenance, and so forth.

Profit or Loss

Profit/loss is the "show me the money" item—the bottom-line takeaway from your income statement. After all the costs and expenses have been deducted from your income, did you make any money?

But remember, your income statement tells you about so much more than just the bottom line.

Let's look at an example to see how (see table 4). This income statement is for XYZ Cleaners for the month of July. Remember, XYZ is a sole proprietorship selling services, not goods. This is a simple income statement that the owner calculates from his deposits and check register.

By looking at revenue, we can see he has three lines of business: dry cleaning, doing regular laundry, and cleaning rugs.

His direct costs (cost of sales) in this business are the cleaning supplies he purchases and wages for himself and one employee. His expenses are payroll taxes, advertising, and the costs of running the store—rent, utilities, and telephone.

XYZ CLEANERS
INCOME STATEMENT FOR THE MONTH OF JULY 2020

REVENUE:	
DRY CLEANING SALES	$5,500
LAUNDRY SALES	$2,000
RUG CLEANING SALES	$1,500
TOTAL SALES	**$9,000**
COST OF SALES:	
CLEANING SOLUTIONS	$1,500
WAGES	$3,800
TOTAL COST OF SALES	(59%) **$5,300**
GROSS MARGIN	(41%) **$3,700**
EXPENSES:	
RENT	$800
UTILITIES	$200
TELEPHONE	$100
ADVERTISING	$200
PAYROLL TAXES	$760
TOTAL EXPENSES	(23%) **$2,060**
PROFIT (LOSS)	(18%) **$1,640**

Table 4. Income statement for XYZ Cleaners

The store had a profit of $1,640 for the month of July. That profit is 18 percent of his sales (take the profit divided by total sales—the figure appears in the far-right column). Whether that's terrible or great depends on the standard for that industry and the goals of the business owner.

PROFIT / TOTAL SALES = PROFIT AS A PERCENT OF SALES
$1,640 / $9,000 = 18 PERCENT

We can also see the makeup of his sales—the total of each category for the month. If we had a few statements from other months to compare this one to, we could tell a lot more, but we'll get into that later. Right now we can see that dry cleaning makes by far the most money.

Look at his cost of sales.

Cost of sales reflects the direct costs of manufacturing the products in your sales section. In our example, the cost of sales includes cleaning solutions and wages for the owner and one employee. The cost of cleaning solutions may be high or low; we don't know from looking at just one month.

But we might wonder, How much cleaning solution is left in the store at the end of the month? And, Is this an average payroll number for the month? Those are the kinds of things to look at in the cost of sales section.

The total cost of sales here is $5,300, which is 59 percent of sales ($5,300 divided by $9,000 sales).

$5,300 / $9,000 = 59 PERCENT

This number tells you that the costs to produce/sell the products is 59 percent of the sales prices. If this number gets too large, the owner may need to look at increasing prices or cutting costs.

Now let's look at gross margin.

In the example, the gross margin is $3,700, which is 41 percent of sales. This leaves 59 percent of sales to cover the rest of the expenses of the cleaners.

What about expenses?

XYZ Cleaners has pretty standard operating costs—rent, utilities, phone, advertising, and payroll taxes. Operating costs are the expenses related to the operation of your business.

When looking at any income statement, you want to look at each expense item and ask yourself if these costs seem reasonable for the location of the business. High-rent districts have higher costs, for instance, but these are usually offset by the higher sales that come with more foot traffic.

Advertising costs should be tracked, and the sales associated with each ad should be tallied.

Payroll taxes should include the employer's share of Social Security and Medicare taxes, as well as unemployment and workers' compensation taxes. This amount will fluctuate as wages change.

Keeping an eye on expenses is just as important as watching your sales. Look at total expenses as a percentage of sales. In the example, total expenses are $2,060, which is 23 percent of sales. Watch this as you go from month to month. If it fluctuates, try to discern why.

Percentage of sales is important because it gives us a measure for each item on our income statement. For example, if rent is 2 percent of our sales, that's a whole lot better than 20 percent. Each expense can be seen as a percent of sales, and that gives us another way to compare monthly activity. If our supplies expense is normally 5 percent of sales, and then one month it jumps to 35 percent, that's something to investigate. The actual dollar figure might not seem out of order, but the percent of sales will.

So, what should you look for? High percentages or low? It depends on your business. You can find industry standards for your business online. Bizstats.com is one place to find them, and you can use them to compare your financials to those of your competitors. This data will normally be given as percent of sales.

That leads us to the last line item, which is profit, or the bottom line.

SALES – COST OF SALES – EXPENSES = PROFIT (OR LOSS)

In our example, the profit is $1,640, which is 18 percent of sales. Some businesses will only see a 2 or 3 percent profit. Again, find out what the norm is in your industry.

Income Statement Summary

What does all this tell you?

We know what sales were for the month of July, and not just in total but in each category. We know which category is the best seller, and which has the lowest sales. By monitoring these numbers (preferably over several months or even a year), we can see which product or service needs to be backed up by more advertising or promotions, and even which ones should be phased out.

We know what the direct costs of our business are. We will know when it decreases or increases by looking at it as a percentage of sales. If that number seems high, we should start trying to decrease costs, increase sales, or raise prices. We know the components that make up our direct costs, such as materials or products, labor, and freight. We also know what it costs just to be in business, whether or not we even make a sale. We still have to pay the rent, the electricity bill, the phone bill, and our employees.

And, finally, we know if, after all this effort, we made or lost money. If we lost money, we know what to do to change that: either increase sales or decrease costs.

Now that you have the basics, let's throw in something else.

Let's stick with XYZ Cleaners, but let's go to the next month, and add a year-to-date column. This is called a comparative income statement (see table 5). Since a lot of income statements have a year-to-date column, it's essential to understand it. This column gives you the accumulated total for the year thus far for each line item. For example, for rent expense, the current month column gives you the rent paid for this month, and the year-to-date column gives you the accumulated rent paid for all the months in the current year so far.

Having these columns side by side allows us to see three things at once: (1) We can see how the company is doing in the current month; (2) We get a quick snapshot of our year-to-date performance; and (3) We're able to put the current month into the larger context of year-to-date performance.

XYZ CLEANERS INCOME STATEMENT FOR THE MONTH OF AUGUST 2020		
	AUGUST	YEAR TO DATE
REVENUE:		
DRY CLEANING SALES	$6,000	$42,000
LAUNDRY SALES	$2,300	$11,000
RUG CLEANING SALES	$900	$8,500
TOTAL REVENUE	$9,200	$61,500
COST OF SALES:		
CLEANING SOLUTIONS	$2,300	$13,600
WAGES	$5,000	$29,000
TOTAL COST OF SALES	(79%) $7,300	(69%) $42,600
GROSS MARGIN	(21%) $1,900	(20%) $18,900
EXPENSES:		
RENT	$800	$6,400
UTILITIES	$220	$1,520
TELEPHONE	$120	$800
ADVERTISING	$400	$1,600
PAYROLL TAXES	$840	$5,800
TOTAL EXPENSES	$2,380	$16,120
PROFIT (LOSS)	$-400	$2,780

Table 5. Comparative income statement for XYZ Cleaners

In reviewing the two columns, you'll probably notice right away that August shows a loss for the month. But also notice that the year-to-date still shows a profit. You'll have good months and bad months, and of course you'll hope that the good ones outweigh the bad. Even so, you should try to figure out why you had a loss. Did your costs go up? Did you buy too much material? Did sales go down?

Look at sales for August. As in the July example, we see total sales and the total of each category. With the addition of the year-to-date column, we can take the year-to-date number and divide by the number of months, eight in this example, to find the average monthly sales. That helps you read the statement better—knowing whether August sales are better or lower than average.

You can do the same calculation for your expenses.

Dry cleaning sales had a better-than-average month ($42,000 / 8 = $5,500), as did laundry sales ($11,000 / 8 = $1,375), but rug cleaning sales had a lower-than-average month ($8,500 / 8 = $1,062).

TOTAL SALES / NUMBER OF MONTHS IN STATEMENT = AVERAGE MONTHLY SALES

This quick exercise illustrates another benefit of watching your income statement month-to-month: You see the seasonality of your business. Retailers peak in December. Pool cleaners peak in the summer months.

For cost of sales in August, each of the direct costs had a higher-than-average month, too. But if sales were higher in August, it stands to reason that costs would be higher, too (at the very least, more sales means more cleaning solution needed). And if wages increased, maybe the owner had to add an employee.

Notice that the cost of sales as a percent of sales is a little higher in August than it is for the year-to-date. Since this business operates on a cash basis, maybe the owner found a sale on cleaning solutions and bought extra.

After sales of $9,200, and cost of sales of $7,300, the business owner has covered his direct costs and has $1,900 left over to cover the other expenses of doing business (overhead).

When we compare July to August, we notice that the rent is the same, utilities and phone went up a little, advertising doubled, and payroll taxes are up.

Above, we thought the owner might have added an employee. This would explain the increase in payroll taxes. You can gather a lot of information like this by comparing month to month.

So after adding up rent, utilities, phone, advertising, and payroll taxes, we have total expenses of $2,380, which gives us a loss of $480.

If the owner wanted to turn that loss into a profit, what could he do? He could increase sales, decrease costs, or raise prices. We have seen which costs went up (cleaning solutions, wages, utilities, and phone), and we've seen which category of sales has decreased (rug cleaning), so we can see the best places to make changes. The owner could advertise his rug cleaning business, since those sales are the lowest. Or he could shop around for better prices on his cleaning solutions or his phone service. Maybe he should raise prices to cover the increase in his costs. The point is that he knows, by using his income statement, where he should focus his efforts.

Let's get a little more involved. We'll look at our other fictional company—Mountain Man Outfitters, a one-owner corporation with stores in three locations. While the owner combined the three locations' data for the company's balance sheet, he broke the numbers down by store location for the income statement. He then summarized them across sales, operating profit, and profit (loss) (see table 6).

Looking at the top of the income statement, we see that it is prepared "for the month ended Dec. 31." So we know that all these numbers are just for the month of December.

Notice there are four columns of data. They separate out the figures for the three different shop locations, allowing the owner to see the income and expenses for each location, as well as the combined total to show how the entire business did for the month (shown as the fourth column, "Total").

This income statement, like all statements of this kind, follows the same pattern we saw above with XYZ Cleaners—revenue, cost of sales, operating profit (called gross margin in the last example), expenses, and finally, profit (loss).

First, take a quick look at the totals—sales, cost of sales, operating profit, expenses, and profit—for each location. Also, note that this income statement shows you the percent of sales for those totals.

Right away you can see that the Breckenridge store has the most sales, and the Boulder store has the least.

MOUNTAIN MAN OUTFITTERS, INC.
INCOME STATEMENT FOR MONTH ENDED DEC. 31, 2020

	BOULDER	DENVER	BRECKENRIDGE	TOTAL
SALES:				
SKIING PRODUCTS	$152,000	$172,000	$188,000	$512,000
HIKING PRODUCTS	108,000	125,000	140,000	373,000
HUNTING PRODUCTS	72,000	80,000	95,000	247,000
WATER SPORT PRODUCTS	45,000	56,000	63,000	164,000
TOTAL SALES	377,000	433,000	486,000	1296,000
LESS RETURNS/DISCOUNTS	-4,500	-6,500	-5,900	-16,900
NET SALES	(100%) 372,500	426,500	480,100	1,279,100
COST OF SALES:				
SKIING PRODUCTS	75,000	85,000	97,000	257,000
HIKING PRODUCTS	68,000	75,000	88,000	231,000
HUNTING PRODUCTS	46,000	55,000	60,000	161,000
WATER SPORT PRODUCTS	27,000	35,000	29,000	91,000
SALES FLOOR WAGES	27,000	40,000	55,000	122,000
MANAGER WAGES	5,800	11,000	12,000	28,800
TOTAL COST OF SALES	(67%) 248,800	(71%) 301,000	(71%) 341,000	(70%) 890,800
GROSS MARGIN	(33%) 123,700	(29%) 125,500	(29%) 139,100	(30%) 388,300
EXPENSES:				
ADMINISTRATIVE WAGES	11,500	13,800	16,100	41,400
OWNER WAGES	6,000	6,000	7,000	19,000
PAYROLL TAXES	12,500	17,750	22,500	52,750
EMPLOYEE BENEFITS	10,350	13,500	16,650	40,500
ADVERTISING	2,300	2,400	2,700	7,400
OFFICE EXPENSES	450	500	700	1,650
EDUCATION	200	300	500	1,000
UTILITIES	3,200	3,400	3,700	10,300
TELEPHONE	550	700	850	2,100
RENT	5,100		6,800	11,900
LEGAL & ACCOUNTING	1,200	1,400	1,800	4,400
INSURANCE	1,400	1,700	2,200	5,300
INTEREST		3,400		3,400
COMPUTER	1,350	1,600	1,900	4,850
REPAIRS/MAINTENANCE	700	900	1,200	2,800
BANK FEES	250	300	500	1,050
PROFESSIONAL FEES	650	700	900	2,250
SUBSCRIPTIONS/DUES	140	150	200	490
PROMOTIONS	800	800	1,200	2,800
TRADE SHOWS	1,800		2,400	4,200
TRAVEL	500		600	1,100
TAXES	4,500	6,000	6,000	16,500
DEPRECIATION	16,800	21,600	21,600	60,000
TOTAL EXPENSES	(22%) 82,240	(23%) 96,900	(25%) 118,000	(23%) 297,140
PROFIT (LOSS)	(11%) 41,460	(7%) 28,600	(4%) 21,100	(7%) 91,160

Table 6. Income statement per location and in total

MOUNTAIN MAN OUTFITTERS, INC.
INCOME STATEMENT FOR MONTH ENDED DEC. 31, 2020

	BOULDER	DENVER	BRECKENRIDGE	TOTAL
SALES:				
SKIING PRODUCTS	$152,000	$172,000	$188,000	$512,000
HIKING PRODUCTS	108,000	125,000	140,000	373,000
HUNTING PRODUCTS	72,000	80,000	95,000	247,000
WATER SPORT PRODUCTS	45,000	56,000	63,000	164,000
TOTAL SALES	377,000	433,000	486,000	1296,000
LESS RETURNS/DISCOUNTS	-4,500	-6,500	-5,900	-16,900
NET SALES	(100%) 372,500	426,500	480,100	1,279,100
COST OF SALES:				
SKIING PRODUCTS	75,000	85,000	97,000	257,000
HIKING PRODUCTS	68,000	75,000	88,000	231,000
HUNTING PRODUCTS	46,000	55,000	60,000	161,000
WATER SPORT PRODUCTS	27,000	35,000	29,000	91,000
SALES FLOOR WAGES	27,000	40,000	55,000	122,000
MANAGER WAGES	5,800	11,000	12,000	28,800
TOTAL COST OF SALES	(67%) 248,800	(71%) 301,000	(71%) 341,000	(70%) 890,800
GROSS MARGIN	(33%) 123,700	(29%) 125,500	(29%) 139,100	(30%) 388,300
EXPENSES:				
ADMINISTRATIVE WAGES	11,500	13,800	16,100	41,400
OWNER WAGES	6,000	6,000	7,000	19,000
PAYROLL TAXES	12,500	17,750	22,500	52,750
EMPLOYEE BENEFITS	10,350	13,500	16,650	40,500
ADVERTISING	2,300	2,400	2,700	7,400
OFFICE EXPENSES	450	500	700	1,650
EDUCATION	200	300	500	1,000
UTILITIES	3,200	3,400	3,700	10,300
TELEPHONE	550	700	850	2,100
RENT	5,100		6,800	11,900
LEGAL & ACCOUNTING	1,200	1,400	1,800	4,400
INSURANCE	1,400	1,700	2,200	5,300
INTEREST		3,400		3,400
COMPUTER	1,350	1,600	1,900	4,850
REPAIRS/MAINTENANCE	700	900	1,200	2,800
BANK FEES	250	300	500	1,050
PROFESSIONAL FEES	650	700	900	2,250
SUBSCRIPTIONS/DUES	140	150	200	490
PROMOTIONS	800	800	1,200	2,800
TRADE SHOWS	1,800		2,400	4,200
TRAVEL	500		600	1,100
TAXES	4,500	6,000	6,000	16,500
DEPRECIATION	16,800	21,600	21,600	60,000
TOTAL EXPENSES	(22%) 82,240	(23%) 96,900	(25%) 118,000	(23%) 297,140
PROFIT (LOSS)	(11%) 41,460	(7%) 28,600	(4%) 21,100	(7%) 91,160

Table 7. Cost of sales on the income statement

Take a look at total cost of sales (see table 7). Though the amounts vary, notice that the Denver and Breckenridge stores have the same percent of sales (71 percent) for their cost of sales, but the Boulder store has a lower cost of sales based on the percent of sales (67 percent) for that figure.

Next look at the operating profit. As expected, based on the cost of sales numbers, the Boulder store has a higher operating profit, since it had a lower cost of sales.

Now look at the company total for operating profit—it's $388,300, or 30 percent of sales. That means the owner has 30 percent of each sale left over to cover other, nondirect, expenses.

Next we turn to total expenses for each store location. They vary in amount for each store, but look at the related percent of sales. Breckenridge, at 25 percent, has the highest expenses as percent of sales—which probably means it's the largest location.

Now let's look at profit, along the bottom. Each store location shows a profit for the month, and the company as a whole made a profit of $91,160—or 7 percent of sales, which is pretty good.

Let's look at the sections of the income statement in more detail. First, we'll look at sales, then cost of sales, then expenses.

MOUNTAIN MAN OUTFITTERS, INC.
INCOME STATEMENT FOR MONTH ENDED DEC. 31, 2020

	BOULDER	DENVER	BRECKENRIDGE	TOTAL
SALES:				
SKIING PRODUCTS	$152,000	$172,000	$188,000	$512,000
HIKING PRODUCTS	108,000	125,000	140,000	373,000
HUNTING PRODUCTS	72,000	80,000	95,000	247,000
WATER SPORT PRODUCTS	45,000	56,000	63,000	164,000
TOTAL SALES	377,000	433,000	486,000	1296,000
LESS RETURNS/DISCOUNTS	-4,500	-6,500	-5,900	-16,900
NET SALES	(100%) 372,500	426,500	480,100	1,279,100
COST OF SALES:				
SKIING PRODUCTS	75,000	85,000	97,000	257,000
HIKING PRODUCTS	68,000	75,000	88,000	231,000
HUNTING PRODUCTS	46,000	55,000	60,000	161,000
WATER SPORT PRODUCTS	27,000	35,000	29,000	91,000
SALES FLOOR WAGES	27,000	40,000	55,000	122,000
MANAGER WAGES	5,800	11,000	12,000	28,800
TOTAL COST OF SALES	(67%) 248,800	(71%) 301,000	(71%) 341,000	(70%) 890,800
GROSS MARGIN	(33%) 123,700	(29%) 125,500	(29%) 139,100	(30%) 388,300
EXPENSES:				
ADMINISTRATIVE WAGES	11,500	13,800	16,100	41,400
OWNER WAGES	6,000	6,000	7,000	19,000
PAYROLL TAXES	12,500	17,750	22,500	52,750
EMPLOYEE BENEFITS	10,350	13,500	16,650	40,500
ADVERTISING	2,300	2,400	2,700	7,400
OFFICE EXPENSES	450	500	700	1,650
EDUCATION	200	300	500	1,000
UTILITIES	3,200	3,400	3,700	10,300
TELEPHONE	550	700	850	2,100
RENT	5,100		6,800	11,900
LEGAL & ACCOUNTING	1,200	1,400	1,800	4,400
INSURANCE	1,400	1,700	2,200	5,300
INTEREST		3,400		3,400
COMPUTER	1,350	1,600	1,900	4,850
REPAIRS/MAINTENANCE	700	900	1,200	2,800
BANK FEES	250	300	500	1,050
PROFESSIONAL FEES	650	700	900	2,250
SUBSCRIPTIONS/DUES	140	150	200	490
PROMOTIONS	800	800	1,200	2,800
TRADE SHOWS	1,800		2,400	4,200
TRAVEL	500		600	1,100
TAXES	4,500	6,000	6,000	16,500
DEPRECIATION	16,800	21,600	21,600	60,000
TOTAL EXPENSES	(22%) 82,240	(23%) 96,900	(25%) 118,000	(23%) 297,140
PROFIT (LOSS)	(11%) 41,460	(7%) 28,600	(4%) 21,100	(7%) 91,160

Table 8. Sales figures by store on the income statement

Sales

Notice how this business owner has organized his sales. He's divided them into product divisions based on activity—skiing, hiking, hunting, and water sports. Maybe his stores have separate departments for each of these activities. He could have split his sales other ways, by different categories like clothing, accessories, gear, etc. but the fact that he did it this way tells us he wanted to track the performance of each of these product categories. When you start preparing your own income statements, spend some time thinking about how you want to analyze your sales, and then structure your categories accordingly.

Looking closely at the sales figure (see table 8) for each store by category, we can see which store sold more product in which category, which is the best seller for the company as a whole, and which store location is the best seller overall. That's a lot of valuable data in just a few lines.

We're also able to confirm a previous hunch about the Breckenridge store—looking at the numbers below, we can safely assume that it is the largest store (in physical size), followed by Denver, and then Boulder. We can deduce that based on sales, cost of sales, and expense numbers.

We have total sales as before, but then we subtract a new item: returns and discounts, which reflects the value of returned and discounted merchandise. If you normally sell a product for $100, but it's an older item so you discount it by 10 percent and sell it for $90, $100 goes to your sales account, and that -$10 goes into the returns and discounts account.

That brings us to the line item of net sales, or total sales "net of" any discounts or returns. And that's the sales figure used to calculate the percent of all sales figures.

MOUNTAIN MAN OUTFITTERS, INC.
INCOME STATEMENT FOR MONTH ENDED DEC. 31, 2020

	BOULDER	DENVER	BRECKENRIDGE	TOTAL
SALES:				
SKIING PRODUCTS	$152,000	$172,000	$188,000	$512,000
HIKING PRODUCTS	108,000	125,000	140,000	373,000
HUNTING PRODUCTS	72,000	80,000	95,000	247,000
WATER SPORT PRODUCTS	45,000	56,000	63,000	164,000
TOTAL SALES	377,000	433,000	486,000	1296,000
LESS RETURNS/DISCOUNTS	-4,500	-6,500	-5,900	-16,900
NET SALES	(100%) 372,500	426,500	480,100	1,279,100
COST OF SALES:				
SKIING PRODUCTS	75,000	85,000	97,000	257,000
HIKING PRODUCTS	68,000	75,000	88,000	231,000
HUNTING PRODUCTS	46,000	55,000	60,000	161,000
WATER SPORT PRODUCTS	27,000	35,000	29,000	91,000
SALES FLOOR WAGES	27,000	40,000	55,000	122,000
MANAGER WAGES	5,800	11,000	12,000	28,800
TOTAL COST OF SALES	(67%) 248,800	(71%) 301,000	(71%) 341,000	(70%) 890,800
GROSS MARGIN	(33%) 123,700	(29%) 125,500	(29%) 139,100	(30%) 388,300
EXPENSES:				
ADMINISTRATIVE WAGES	11,500	13,800	16,100	41,400
OWNER WAGES	6,000	6,000	7,000	19,000
PAYROLL TAXES	12,500	17,750	22,500	52,750
EMPLOYEE BENEFITS	10,350	13,500	16,650	40,500
ADVERTISING	2,300	2,400	2,700	7,400
OFFICE EXPENSES	450	500	700	1,650
EDUCATION	200	300	500	1,000
UTILITIES	3,200	3,400	3,700	10,300
TELEPHONE	550	700	850	2,100
RENT	5,100		6,800	11,900
LEGAL & ACCOUNTING	1,200	1,400	1,800	4,400
INSURANCE	1,400	1,700	2,200	5,300
INTEREST		3,400		3,400
COMPUTER	1,350	1,600	1,900	4,850
REPAIRS/MAINTENANCE	700	900	1,200	2,800
BANK FEES	250	300	500	1,050
PROFESSIONAL FEES	650	700	900	2,250
SUBSCRIPTIONS/DUES	140	150	200	490
PROMOTIONS	800	800	1,200	2,800
TRADE SHOWS	1,800		2,400	4,200
TRAVEL	500		600	1,100
TAXES	4,500	6,000	6,000	16,500
DEPRECIATION	16,800	21,600	21,600	60,000
TOTAL EXPENSES	(22%) 82,240	(23%) 96,900	(25%) 118,000	(23%) 297,140
PROFIT (LOSS)	(11%) 41,460	(7%) 28,600	(4%) 21,100	(7%) 91,160

Table 9. Cost of sales by activity on the income statement

Cost of Sales

This is the direct costs of your sales, and for a retail operation the largest cost is always the cost of selling your products. This owner has separated out his costs by the same activity categories he used for his sales.

Looking at this section (see table 9), you can tell which activity category has the highest costs, per store, and for the whole company. Skiing products have the highest cost, but they also have the highest sales. Next comes hiking, then hunting, then water sports.

You could calculate individual operating profits per activity category based on these numbers. For example, take skiing sales less skiing costs, and you get the operating profit for that category.

We have two more items in the cost of sales section—sales floor wages and manager wages. These wages are a direct cost of selling, so they belong in this section. Later on, we'll see that other wages are listed in the expenses category.

You can see the higher wage costs belong to Breckenridge, the largest store. That makes sense, since there is more square footage in the store and more products, requiring more sales personnel.

After total cost of sales we have operating profit, which is net sales minus total cost of sales.

Again, we can see the numbers for each store and for the company as a whole. The owner can look at operating profit to see how each store is doing every month, and how much each store contributes to the business as a whole. This is valuable information that informs his business planning, marketing, and financial projections.

If he watches his income statements each month, he will notice when a store location seems to be slipping or having low sales, or when its costs are increasing, and can start addressing the issues right away.

That's the main purpose of financial statements—to show you, the business owner, how the business is doing. When there's a negative change, you'll see it right away and have time to do something about it.

Now let's look at the next category, expenses (see table 10).

MOUNTAIN MAN OUTFITTERS, INC.
INCOME STATEMENT FOR MONTH ENDED DEC. 31, 2020

	BOULDER	DENVER	BRECKENRIDGE	TOTAL
SALES:				
SKIING PRODUCTS	$152,000	$172,000	$188,000	$512,000
HIKING PRODUCTS	108,000	125,000	140,000	373,000
HUNTING PRODUCTS	72,000	80,000	95,000	247,000
WATER SPORT PRODUCTS	45,000	56,000	63,000	164,000
TOTAL SALES	377,000	433,000	486,000	1296,000
LESS RETURNS/DISCOUNTS	-4,500	-6,500	-5,900	-16,900
NET SALES	(100%) 372,500	426,500	480,100	1,279,100
COST OF SALES:				
SKIING PRODUCTS	75,000	85,000	97,000	257,000
HIKING PRODUCTS	68,000	75,000	88,000	231,000
HUNTING PRODUCTS	46,000	55,000	60,000	161,000
WATER SPORT PRODUCTS	27,000	35,000	29,000	91,000
SALES FLOOR WAGES	27,000	40,000	55,000	122,000
MANAGER WAGES	5,800	11,000	12,000	28,800
TOTAL COST OF SALES	(67%) 248,800	(71%) 301,000	(71%) 341,000	(70%) 890,800
GROSS MARGIN	(33%) 123,700	(29%) 125,500	(29%) 139,100	(30%) 388,300
EXPENSES:				
ADMINISTRATIVE WAGES	11,500	13,800	16,100	41,400
OWNER WAGES	6,000	6,000	7,000	19,000
PAYROLL TAXES	12,500	17,750	22,500	52,750
EMPLOYEE BENEFITS	10,350	13,500	16,650	40,500
ADVERTISING	2,300	2,400	2,700	7,400
OFFICE EXPENSES	450	500	700	1,650
EDUCATION	200	300	500	1,000
UTILITIES	3,200	3,400	3,700	10,300
TELEPHONE	550	700	850	2,100
RENT	5,100		6,800	11,900
LEGAL & ACCOUNTING	1,200	1,400	1,800	4,400
INSURANCE	1,400	1,700	2,200	5,300
INTEREST		3,400		3,400
COMPUTER	1,350	1,600	1,900	4,850
REPAIRS/MAINTENANCE	700	900	1,200	2,800
BANK FEES	250	300	500	1,050
PROFESSIONAL FEES	650	700	900	2,250
SUBSCRIPTIONS/DUES	140	150	200	490
PROMOTIONS	800	800	1,200	2,800
TRADE SHOWS	1,800		2,400	4,200
TRAVEL	500		600	1,100
TAXES	4,500	6,000	6,000	16,500
DEPRECIATION	16,800	21,600	21,600	60,000
TOTAL EXPENSES	(22%) 82,240	(23%) 96,900	(25%) 118,000	(23%) 297,140
PROFIT (LOSS)	(11%) 41,460	(7%) 28,600	(4%) 21,100	(7%) 91,160

Table 10. Expenses on the income statement

Expenses

The first expense is administrative wages. This item reflects the nonsales employee wages, such as secretaries, bookkeepers, janitors, the IT person, and the marketing manager.

Next, we see the owner's wages. It looks as if he's allocating his wages to each store, maybe on the basis of how much time he spends at each.

Then we have the payroll taxes for all the wages. Payroll taxes include the employer's share of Social Security and Medicare taxes, federal and state unemployment taxes, and any workers' compensation taxes. This figure should fluctuate with total wages. If wages are up, there will be more taxes.

Employee benefits is listed next. This would normally include medical and dental insurance premiums, any company-match payments for pension plans, and any life and disability plan premiums.

Then we have advertising costs. You can see which store pays more or less for its advertising. Often, it varies by location, since larger metropolitan areas tend to have higher advertising rates than small towns. Also, the type of advertising—newspaper, billboard, flyers—will affect the pricing.

Next come office expenses, which reflect each store's purchase of office supplies—pens, paper, folders, ink cartridges, and so on. Notice that the amounts for this line item increase with the size of the store.

Education is next. This would reflect classes, webinars, and anything else that helps employees do their jobs, keep certifications, or advance within the company.

Utilities and telephone are the next two expense items. Obviously the utility costs vary by store size, and the telephone expense would vary by the store activity level. The larger store would have more employees and need more phones, and the busier the store, the more incoming calls and the more employee activity inside the store.

Next we have rent. Notice that only two stores have rent. That means the Denver store is owned by the company. Drop down three lines to interest. Notice that only the Denver location has that expense. That reflects the interest portion of any loans, which would be the mortgage payment. So in this example, the three stores have either (1) a rent payment, but no mortgage payment (which would include interest), or (2) a mortgage payment (which includes interest), but no rent payment.

Next we have legal and accounting. The legal and accounting expense reflects accounting fees paid to the company's CPA firm, and toward any legal issues they may have. Notice that the figures are fairly small, so the store probably doesn't have any major legal problems this month. The wages paid to the company's bookkeeper or accountant would be reflected in the administrative wages section.

If a company did not have a bookkeeper or accountant on the payroll, and instead hired an outside accountant to keep the books, then those service fees would be reflected here on the legal and accounting expense line.

The next expense line is insurance. These amounts reflect each store's need for commercial insurance coverage. Each store's premium is different, so either each store has its own coverage, or the owner has a policy covering all locations and he splits the premium costs per location on his income statement.

After interest expense comes computer expense. This would *not* be the costs of the computers in the store; that would be an asset. This cost reflects any computer services the company needs, such as IT repair and support or the installation of new software.

Repairs and maintenance expense includes cleaning the stores and offices, maintaining the outside of the buildings, keeping the sidewalks tidy, and so on. For the two leased stores, the costs that would be the lessee's responsibility would depend on the contract. Some expenses would be the responsibility of the building owner.

Any large remodeling costs for the inside of the leased stores would be posted to a leasehold improvements account, which is an asset, and would be shown on the balance sheet.

Bank fees, the next item, includes any service fees associated with checking or savings accounts, or any loan fees (separate from interest).

Professional fees is kind of a catchall for any other services besides legal and accounting or computer services. Generally, we would see consulting fees (computer services, software updates, sales consulting), decorator fees, or other similar expenses in this line.

Subscriptions and dues includes any professional club dues, local chamber of commerce dues, professional publications, or any similar items that are business related.

Promotions is similar to advertising, but covers the costs of promoting the business in any sale event. Suppose this business owner had a large sale at each store, putting up tents in the parking lot and bringing an elephant to each store to attract shoppers. That's a promotion (and a crazy idea!).

This owner chose to list trade shows as a separate line item (see table 11). Notice that only the two leased locations have that expense. The main store does not participate.

MOUNTAIN MAN OUTFITTERS, INC.
INCOME STATEMENT FOR MONTH ENDED DEC. 31, 2020

	BOULDER	DENVER	BRECKENRIDGE	TOTAL
SALES:				
SKIING PRODUCTS	$152,000	$172,000	$188,000	$512,000
HIKING PRODUCTS	108,000	125,000	140,000	373,000
HUNTING PRODUCTS	72,000	80,000	95,000	247,000
WATER SPORT PRODUCTS	45,000	56,000	63,000	164,000
TOTAL SALES	377,000	433,000	486,000	1296,000
LESS RETURNS/DISCOUNTS	-4,500	-6,500	-5,900	-16,900
NET SALES	(100%) 372,500	426,500	480,100	1,279,100
COST OF SALES:				
SKIING PRODUCTS	75,000	85,000	97,000	257,000
HIKING PRODUCTS	68,000	75,000	88,000	231,000
HUNTING PRODUCTS	46,000	55,000	60,000	161,000
WATER SPORT PRODUCTS	27,000	35,000	29,000	91,000
SALES FLOOR WAGES	27,000	40,000	55,000	122,000
MANAGER WAGES	5,800	11,000	12,000	28,800
TOTAL COST OF SALES	(67%) 248,800	(71%) 301,000	(71%) 341,000	(70%) 890,800
GROSS MARGIN	(33%) 123,700	(29%) 125,500	(29%) 139,100	(30%) 388,300
EXPENSES:				
ADMINISTRATIVE WAGES	11,500	13,800	16,100	41,400
OWNER WAGES	6,000	6,000	7,000	19,000
PAYROLL TAXES	12,500	17,750	22,500	52,750
EMPLOYEE BENEFITS	10,350	13,500	16,650	40,500
ADVERTISING	2,300	2,400	2,700	7,400
OFFICE EXPENSES	450	500	700	1,650
EDUCATION	200	300	500	1,000
UTILITIES	3,200	3,400	3,700	10,300
TELEPHONE	550	700	850	2,100
RENT	5,100		6,800	11,900
LEGAL & ACCOUNTING	1,200	1,400	1,800	4,400
INSURANCE	1,400	1,700	2,200	5,300
INTEREST		3,400		3,400
COMPUTER	1,350	1,600	1,900	4,850
REPAIRS/MAINTENANCE	700	900	1,200	2,800
BANK FEES	250	300	500	1,050
PROFESSIONAL FEES	650	700	900	2,250
SUBSCRIPTIONS/DUES	140	150	200	490
PROMOTIONS	800	800	1,200	2,800
TRADE SHOWS	1,800		2,400	4,200
TRAVEL	500		600	1,100
TAXES	4,500	6,000	6,000	16,500
DEPRECIATION	16,800	21,600	21,600	60,000
TOTAL EXPENSES	(22%) 82,240	(23%) 96,900	(25%) 118,000	(23%) 297,140
PROFIT (LOSS)	(11%) 41,460	(7%) 28,600	(4%) 21,100	(7%) 91,160

Table 11. Store-specific expenses on the income statement

Travel expense is for business-only travel. In this case, this line item reflects the costs of traveling to trade shows. It could also include travel to classes or seminars.

Then we have taxes, which would include the cost of any property or real estate taxes paid at each location.

The last expense item is depreciation. Depreciation is a noncash, paper-only expense. It is calculated according to IRS-specified methods. Each plant asset—buildings, vehicles, building or leasehold improvements, furniture and fixtures, computer or office equipment—has what's called a "class." That class might be 31-year real property (buildings) or seven-year property (equipment).

These assets are posted on the books at their actual cost. Then each month, or sometimes only at year-end, you expense a portion of that cost through depreciation. In the previous section on balance sheets, we saw how the asset cost, less any depreciation, equals the net value that we call book value. This term is used exclusively for assets and tells you what the "real value" of an asset is, at any given time, no matter its age. With a glance you know the estimated book value of that asset at its stage of life, be it one year old or 20 years old.

Now that you've looked at each expense, notice the line item of total expenses. This amount is calculated for each store, and for the entire company for the month. The total expenses companywide is $297,140. This is 23 percent of the net sales for this month. Each store's total expenses figure is very close to this number, 22 percent for Boulder, 25 percent for Breckenridge, and the Denver store matches exactly at 23 percent.

Then we see the bottom-line figure: profit (see table 12). Each store has a profit, and the company as a whole shows a profit as well. Notice here, too, the numbers vary with store size and location.

The Boulder store has the lowest sales, the lowest cost of sales, the highest operating profit, the lowest total expenses, and the highest profit. Although this is the smallest store, it has enough sales to cover its costs and expenses, which are kept to a minimum, and enough left over for a handsome profit.

The Denver store is the midsize store, but also the only store that is owned by the company. Its sales are in the middle, so to speak, and so are its cost of sales, operating profit, expenses, and profit.

Then we have the Breckenridge store, the largest, which has the largest sales but *not* the highest profit. A larger store almost always incurs more expenses and costs—but it still contributes a profit to the enterprise.

The owner of this company has a lot to keep track of and probably has an accountant or manager to help him. He should monitor his income statement each month and look for any variations or variances in the percentages.

MOUNTAIN MAN OUTFITTERS, INC.
INCOME STATEMENT FOR MONTH ENDED DEC. 31, 2020

	BOULDER	DENVER	BRECKENRIDGE	TOTAL
SALES:				
SKIING PRODUCTS	$152,000	$172,000	$188,000	$512,000
HIKING PRODUCTS	108,000	125,000	140,000	373,000
HUNTING PRODUCTS	72,000	80,000	95,000	247,000
WATER SPORT PRODUCTS	45,000	56,000	63,000	164,000
TOTAL SALES	377,000	433,000	486,000	1296,000
LESS RETURNS/DISCOUNTS	-4,500	-6,500	-5,900	-16,900
NET SALES	(100%) 372,500	426,500	480,100	1,279,100
COST OF SALES:				
SKIING PRODUCTS	75,000	85,000	97,000	257,000
HIKING PRODUCTS	68,000	75,000	88,000	231,000
HUNTING PRODUCTS	46,000	55,000	60,000	161,000
WATER SPORT PRODUCTS	27,000	35,000	29,000	91,000
SALES FLOOR WAGES	27,000	40,000	55,000	122,000
MANAGER WAGES	5,800	11,000	12,000	28,800
TOTAL COST OF SALES	(67%) 248,800	(71%) 301,000	(71%) 341,000	(70%) 890,800
GROSS MARGIN	(33%) 123,700	(29%) 125,500	(29%) 139,100	(30%) 388,300
EXPENSES:				
ADMINISTRATIVE WAGES	11,500	13,800	16,100	41,400
OWNER WAGES	6,000	6,000	7,000	19,000
PAYROLL TAXES	12,500	17,750	22,500	52,750
EMPLOYEE BENEFITS	10,350	13,500	16,650	40,500
ADVERTISING	2,300	2,400	2,700	7,400
OFFICE EXPENSES	450	500	700	1,650
EDUCATION	200	300	500	1,000
UTILITIES	3,200	3,400	3,700	10,300
TELEPHONE	550	700	850	2,100
RENT	5,100		6,800	11,900
LEGAL & ACCOUNTING	1,200	1,400	1,800	4,400
INSURANCE	1,400	1,700	2,200	5,300
INTEREST		3,400		3,400
COMPUTER	1,350	1,600	1,900	4,850
REPAIRS/MAINTENANCE	700	900	1,200	2,800
BANK FEES	250	300	500	1,050
PROFESSIONAL FEES	650	700	900	2,250
SUBSCRIPTIONS/DUES	140	150	200	490
PROMOTIONS	800	800	1,200	2,800
TRADE SHOWS	1,800		2,400	4,200
TRAVEL	500		600	1,100
TAXES	4,500	6,000	6,000	16,500
DEPRECIATION	16,800	21,600	21,600	60,000
TOTAL EXPENSES	(22%) 82,240	(23%) 96,900	(25%) 118,000	(23%) 297,140
PROFIT (LOSS)	(11%) 41,460	(7%) 28,600	(4%) 21,100	(7%) 91,160

Table 12. Profit (loss) on the income statement

If one store suddenly has a 5 percent increase in cost, for example, the owner would want to figure out why. The same would hold true if another store's sales decreased by 10 percent.

An income statement is not a stagnant piece of paper. It is a "live" monitor of business. Changes can be red flags, or they can signify a positive trend, such as an increase in sales or a decrease in cost. Still, a small business owner should know *why* sales increased or costs decreased. More experienced or savvy owners will even be able to predict the changes before they see the statement.

Everything you do in your small business will be reflected in your income statement. If you have a 20 percent off sale, and had a great day of sales because of it, that will show up on your income statement. If you raised prices, that will be reflected, too. It might show up as increased sales because of the higher per-item price, *or* it may translate to lower sales because a price hike meant less volume sold.

For all these reasons, it's vital to monitor your income statement regularly.

We have now looked at a simple income statement, a comparative income statement showing the current month and the year-to-date figures, and a more complex income statement showing multiple locations.

This leads us to the third financial statement—the statement of cash flows.

THE STATEMENT OF CASH FLOWS

The statement of cash flows is used mainly by larger corporations that use the accrual method of accounting. To review, this method specifies that all revenue is realized (posted) when sold, not when money is received, and that all expenses are realized (posted) when incurred, not when they are paid. The accrual method is used so that revenue and expenses are more closely matched (the matching principle of GAAP).

Most small businesses use the cash method, in which revenue is realized (posted) when the money is received and expenses are realized (posted) when paid.

The statement of cash flows is still worth looking at and understanding, even for small business owners who use the cash method.

The statement covers a period of time, just as the income statement does. It transitions the company's finances from an accrual method to the cash method, which gives the business owner an accurate picture of cash going into and out of the company during this time period. It starts with your profit or loss, and brings it back to a cash basis by adding or subtracting business activity that uses cash but hasn't been reflected on the income statement. This could be principal paid on loans, accounts receivable collected, accounts payable paid, and so forth. The statement ends with the calculation of the cash added to or used by the company.

The statement of cash flows highlights the difference between cash transactions and noncash transactions. Cash transactions are business transactions that affect cash, such as receipts of cash, bills paid by check, bank service charges, and petty cash disbursements.

Noncash transactions are business transactions that do not affect cash, such as owner contributions of equipment, materials purchased on credit (accounts payable), and sales made on credit (accounts receivable).

The statement of cash flows serves to bring all these cash transactions into one report.

A cash flows statement has three sections. Let's look at each section of the statement for Mountain Man Outfitters—first as an overview (see table 13) and then in more detail (table 14).

MOUNTAIN MAN OUTFITTERS, INC.
STATEMENT OF CASH FLOWS FOR MONTH ENDED DEC. 31, 2020

CASH ADDED (USED) BY OPERATING ACTIVITIES:		
OPERATING PROFIT (AKA GROSS MARGIN)	$388,300	
LESS EXPENSES	-297,140	
PROFIT	91,160	
ADD BACK DEPRECIATION	60,000	
INCREASE IN PAYABLES	12,300	
INCREASE IN RECEIVABLES	-25,000	
INCREASE IN INVENTORY	-105,000	
CASH ADDED (USED) BY OPERATING ACTIVITIES		$33,460
CASH ADDED (USED) BY FINANCING ACTIVITIES:		
DECREASE IN LOAN PRINCIPAL	-50,400	
CASH ADDED (USED) BY FINANCING ACTIVIITES		-50,400
CASH ADDED (USED) BY INVESTING ACTIVITIES:		
DIVIDENDS PAID	-200,000	
CASH ADDED (USED) BY INVESTING ACTIVITIES		-200,000
TOTAL CASH USED		$-216,940
CASH BALANCE – BEGINNING JAN. 1, 2020	$631,940	
CASH BALANCE – ENDING DEC. 31, 2020	-$415,000	
CASH USED DURING PERIOD	216,940	

Table 13. Statement of cash flows for Mountain Man Outfitters

Cash from Operating Activities

This section lists the revenue minus the expenses, then nets them to get the profit or loss for the time period covered by the statement of cash flows. Remember, Revenue – Expenses = Profit (Loss). This is the net cash brought into the company from operations. It is essential that the company bring in enough funds to cover its operations without having to take out loans or the owner having to contribute personal funds.

Cash from Financing Activities

In this section you will see the principal portion paid on any loans, and any moneys received from new loans.

Cash from Investing Activities

Included in this section are any investments in other companies, cash put into or taken out of any financial investment funds, and so on. Any owner contributions or payments would also be in this section. These items affect cash, but are not on the income statement.

Then we have a line item as the summary of the above calculations:

Total Cash Added to (Used by) the Organization

This line item is the sum of all the above sections, with each summarized with a total "cash added" or "cash used" figure. Total cash used means cash spent. Total cash added means cash received into the company.

This line shows you the total cash that was accumulated during the month, or the amount of cash decrease for the month. It's usually titled "total cash used" or "total cash added."

Then we have a final small section:

Beginning and Ending Cash Balances

After the above line item, you will see the balance in the cash account at the beginning of the month (or quarter or year) listed, followed by the cash balance at the end of the month (or quarter or year), with the change in cash calculated. This will match the above cash added to/used by the organization number.

Let's look at the statement again (see table 14).

Here we have the three sections: cash from operating activities, cash from financing activities, and cash from investing activities. Note that the heading of the

MOUNTAIN MAN OUTFITTERS, INC.		
STATEMENT OF CASH FLOWS FOR MONTH ENDED DEC. 31, 2020		
CASH ADDED (USED) BY OPERATING ACTIVITIES:		
OPERATING PROFIT (AKA GROSS MARGIN)	$388,300	
LESS EXPENSES	-297,140	
PROFIT	91,160	
ADD BACK DEPRECIATION	60,000	
INCREASE IN PAYABLES	12,300	
INCREASE IN RECEIVABLES	-25,000	
INCREASE IN INVENTORY	-105,000	
CASH ADDED (USED) BY OPERATING ACTIVITIES		$33,460
CASH ADDED (USED) BY FINANCING ACTIVITIES:		
DECREASE IN LOAN PRINCIPAL	-50,400	
CASH ADDED (USED) BY FINANCING ACTIVIITES		-50,400
CASH ADDED (USED) BY INVESTING ACTIVITIES:		
DIVIDENDS PAID	-200,000	
CASH ADDED (USED) BY INVESTING ACTIVITIES		-200,000
TOTAL CASH USED		$-216,940
CASH BALANCE – BEGINNING JAN. 1, 2020	$631,940	
CASH BALANCE – ENDING DEC. 31, 2020	-$415,000	
CASH USED DURING PERIOD	216,940	

Table 14. Sections of the cash flow statement

statement says "for the month ended Dec. 31," meaning that all these activities are for that time period only. The profit (loss) is for the month of December.

Now look at the beginning and ending cash balances—the difference in those two amounts equal the $216,940 in cash used.

Let's take a closer look at each section (see table 14).

Cash Added (Used) by Operating Activities

In this section we start with operating profit (or gross margin, which is our revenue, less cost of goods sold) less expenses, which gives us our profit for the month ending on December 31.

Then we add or subtract balance sheet items that affect cash. But first we add back depreciation. This is included as an expense on the income statement, but it's what's called a "paper transaction" and doesn't affect cash, so we're adding it back.

Next we add in an increase in payables. When we post a voucher for a bill that's due next month, we post that corresponding expense now. That increases what we owe but does not use cash. This does, however, decrease our profit, which is why we add it back in now. We need to know if it affects profit because we've started this statement with our profit (loss), so if an item affects profit (loss) we've already accounted for it. We're only concerned with adding items that have not been accounted for in our profit (loss) from our income statement.

Now we subtract an increase in receivables. When we post a receivable, that means we didn't get cash; we got a promise of payment at a later date. However, when we post a receivable we also post revenue, which increases our profit. The point of our statement of cash flows is to get back to cash, so we need to subtract the increase in receivables out of our profit because we did not receive the cash.

Next we subtract an increase in inventory. When we increase our inventory that means we have purchased products that have not yet been sold. This uses our cash, but is not reflected on the income statement as an expense. Rather, it shows up on the balance sheet as inventory. We subtract it from our profit because it used our cash.

MOUNTAIN MAN OUTFITTERS, INC.
STATEMENT OF CASH FLOWS FOR MONTH ENDED DEC. 31, 2020

CASH ADDED (USED) BY OPERATING ACTIVITIES:		
OPERATING PROFIT (AKA GROSS MARGIN)	$388,300	
LESS EXPENSES	-297,140	
PROFIT	91,160	
ADD BACK DEPRECIATION	60,000	
INCREASE IN PAYABLES	12,300	
INCREASE IN RECEIVABLES	-25,000	
INCREASE IN INVENTORY	-105,000	
CASH ADDED (USED) BY OPERATING ACTIVITIES		$33,460
CASH ADDED (USED) BY FINANCING ACTIVITIES:		
DECREASE IN LOAN PRINCIPAL	-50,400	
CASH ADDED (USED) BY FINANCING ACTIVIITES		-50,400
CASH ADDED (USED) BY INVESTING ACTIVITIES:		
DIVIDENDS PAID	-200,000	
CASH ADDED (USED) BY INVESTING ACTIVITIES		-200,000
TOTAL CASH USED		$-216,940
CASH BALANCE – BEGINNING JAN. 1, 2020	$631,940	
CASH BALANCE – ENDING DEC. 31, 2020	-$415,000	
CASH USED DURING PERIOD	216,940	

Table 15. Cash flows statement: cash added (used) by financing activities

Now we total these numbers up and get a cash added by operations of $33,460.

This means that the actual running of the business produced an increase in cash of $33,460 for the month ending December 31.

Cash Added (Used) by Financing Activities

The only item this business has for this section is a decrease in loan principal. In other words, the business made their loan payments, and the interest showed up in interest expense on the income statement. The principal amount of the payment went on the balance sheet. But it did use cash, so we're subtracting it.

Cash Added (Used) by Investing Activities

The only item we see in this section is dividends paid of $200,000. This was used cash, but was posted to the balance sheet, so we subtract it here, because, as you remember, we're trying to get that profit back to cash.

Now we have the totals for each section, and the grand total of all sections. This is our total cash used of $216,940.

Let's look again at the end of the statement of cash flows. You see listed the beginning and ending cash balances, and the difference between the two, which represents the change in cash for this time period. This change is a negative $216,940, which matches the total cash used figure from the above calculations. This is good since you want the numbers to match.

It would be better to see a positive cash added to the organization rather than a negative one, but let's look at why there's a negative cash used.

Maybe you bought too much inventory. Maybe you need to collect your receivables faster. Then there's the dividends paid, which accounts for most of the cash used.

So this statement of cash flows shows you where your cash is coming from, and where it went. Did your cash flow out of operations, or was it from a loan or investment?

Did your cash get used mostly in operations, was it used to pay down debt, or did you invest some of your cash? Or did you pay it out to the owner by way of a distribution?

This statement will tell you all that.

THE STATEMENT OF RETAINED EARNINGS

This statement calculates the changes in retained earnings. Remember, retained earnings is the accumulated profits and losses for the history of the company (from the date of its inception). The statement of retained earnings is used primarily by large, publicly traded corporations, so many small business owners will never see or use it.

This statement shows the beginning balance in the retained earnings account, then adds in profit, deducts any dividends paid, and then shows the ending balance in retained earnings.

It looks like this (see table 16).

A corporation's retained earnings information is key to its dividends disbursements, year-end closeout process, and company valuation, among other accounting activities. We'll discuss these in greater detail in chapter 5.

JUDY'S MEGALOPOLIS INC. STATEMENT OF RETAINED EARNINGS FOR THE YEAR ENDING 12-31-2020	
RETAINED EARNINGS AT DEC 1, 2020	$150,000
NET INCOME FOR THE YEAR 2020	40,000
DIVIDENDS PAID TO SHAREHOLDERS	-25,000
RETAINED EARNINGS AT DEC 31, 2020	$165,000

Table 16. Statement of retained earnings for Judy's Megalopolis

In this chapter we covered the basic terms, concepts, and statements you'll need in order to understand your business's accounting. Now that we've gone over all the individual pieces, let's put them into the context of your business. In the next chapter we'll look at getting your accounting system set up, implemented, and running.

2

///////////////////////

BUSINESS SETUP

When you start a small business, there are a lot of things to worry about, such as inventory and production, or scheduling jobs and paying bills. Will your business be a corporation that issues stock? Will you have to borrow money to finance start-up costs? How many employees will you need? With all these questions to answer, many new owners aren't sure what to do about accounting (and ironically, accounting is an integral part of the answers to all these questions). A lot of owners mistakenly think that a checkbook is a proper accounting system.

It's not.

The system you choose should be one that makes the process as easy and intuitive as possible so that you keep up with accounting duties. It can be relatively simple, or it can be more complex in how it's set up and what it delivers—it all depends on your needs. Whatever system you go with, you'll need to be able to keep track of all the money coming in and going out of your business.

The largest differentiator between systems is whether they're manual or computerized. In a manual system, you use an assortment of "journals"—either on paper or simple spreadsheets—and make entries manually for every transaction. Computerized systems and software do all the calculations for you, but entail a bit more of a learning curve at the start. Either is fine for a beginning small business, but once you get going you're going to want a computerized system just for the ease and benefits of having it automatically add or subtract customer payments from the total owed and keep running totals of sales and expenses.

We're going to look at a few transactions below in terms of journal entries. But first let's discuss the accounting cycle.

THE ACCOUNTING CYCLE

Every business transaction (a sale, a purchase, paying a bill) is recorded in an accounting journal. At the end of an accounting period (month, quarter, year) the entries are summarized and posted (moved, transferred) into a ledger, and then summarized. The balances in the ledger are then listed in a financial statement.

Accountants use many types of journals—cash disbursement, cash receipts, payroll, general (noncash transactions), and sales. With the advent of the computer and accounting software programs, almost no one uses journal books anymore. The computer automatically summarizes all transactions into journals and posts these totals into a general ledger for you.

Actually, your checkbook is a cash journal. Many people use Excel spreadsheets to keep track of their sales, checks, and deposits. This spreadsheet would then be an accounting journal.

The phrase "posting a journal entry" just means writing down the transaction into a journal—or spreadsheet. A journal entry always has two sides: a debit and a credit. For example, when you pay your electric bill, you have two sides to the transaction—a decrease in cash and an increase in utilities expense.

Remember the accounting equation? The left side (assets) has debit balances, and the right side (liabilities and equity) has credit balances. Debits and credits are simply the transactions that make up the flow of money into and out of your business.

In the examples below, you'll see that both sides of the transaction—the debit and the credit—are included. Don't let this intimidate you; it just means that there are two sides to every business transaction.

You wouldn't actually write your journal entries out like this, but we'll go step-by-step below just for the sake of illustration. In reality, you would just add a transaction in your checkbook ledger for the electric bill you just paid.

Let's look at some business transactions and see how they affect accounting.

Say you started a business checking account with $3,000 in personal funds. This goes into your general journal (paper or computerized), with the following debit and credit entries. Again, the accounting equation stipulates that a debit must equal a credit. So in this case:

DEBIT: CASH IN CHECKING	$3,000
CREDIT: OWNER'S EQUITY	$3,000

This is the journal entry made for a sole proprietor and would show up on your balance sheet.

An S corporation owner would post that initial investment as a loan from the business to her. She gave the company money, so it owes her that money back.

DEBIT: CASH IN CHECKING	$3,000
CREDIT: STOCKHOLDER LOAN	$3,000

On a Balance Sheet these transactions would be included in the above accounts, as shown below.

BALANCE SHEET AS OF MARCH 31, 2020	
CASH IN CHECKING	$5,600
ACCOUNTS RECEIVABLE	$25,000
INVENTORY	$4,500
PREPAID INSURANCE	$3,000
PREPAID TAXES	$1,300
UNEARNED REVENUE	$800
OFFICE EQUIPMENT	$1,800
EQUIPMENT	$6,000
VEHICLES	$26,000
BUILDING & IMPROVEMENTS	$201,000
LESS ACCUMULATED DEPRECIATION	$-20,000
TOTAL ASSETS	$255,000
ACCOUNTS PAYABLE	$2,800
SALES TAX PAYABLE	$1,200
PAYROLL TAXES PAYABLE	
FICA/FEDERAL WITHHOLDING	$3,100
STATE WITHHOLDING	$1,200
LOCAL WITHHOLDING	$600
401(K) WITHHOLDING	$200
EMPLOYEE HEALTH WITHHOLDING	$900
CREDIT CARD PAYABLE	$1,500
VEHICLE LOAN PAYABLE	$4,000
BUILDING LOAN PAYABLE	$1,000
STOCKHOLDER LOAN	$165,000
NOTE PAYABLE OWNER	$40,000
TOTAL LIABILITIES	$222,300
OWNERS EQUITY:	
COMMON STOCK	$500
PREFERRED STOCK	$2,200
RETAINED EARNINGS	$60,000
DIVIDENDS	$-30,000
TOTAL EQUITY	$32,700
TOTAL LIABILITIES & EQUITY	$255,000

INCOME STATEMENT FOR MONTH ENDED MARCH 31, 2020	
SALES	$300,000
SALES RETURNS & ALLOWANCES	$-15,000
NET SALES	$285,000
INTEREST INCOME	$100
TOTAL REVENUE	$285,100
COST OF GOODS SOLD:	
MATERIALS	$114,000
PURCHASES RETURNS	$-1,500
SUBCONTRACT	$36,000
TOTAL COGS	$148,500
GROSS MARGIN	$136,600
EXPENSES:	
ADVERTISING EXPENSE	$6,500
RENT EXPENSE	$3,800
FEDERAL INCOME TAX EXPENSE	$600
INSURANCE EXPENSE	$3,500
UTILITIES EXPENSE	$6,000
DUES & SUBSCRIPTIONS EXPENSE	$2,000
GROSS WAGES	$78,000
EMPLOYEE DISABILITY INS. EXP.	$1,400
FICA EXPENSE	$5,355
FEDERAL UNEMPLOYMENT EXP.	$1,100
STATE UNEMPLOYMENT EXPENSE	$1,300
EMPLOYEE HEALTH INS. EXPENSE	$4,000
INTEREST EXPENSE	$6,000
BAD DEBT EXPENSE	$2,000
DEPRECIATION EXPENSE	$6,000
TOTAL EXPENSES	$127,555
PROFIT/LOSS	$9,045

MAKING JOURNAL ENTRIES

Now let's take a quick look at how debit and credit transactions are entered into a journal. If you're using a manual accounting system, you'll need a pad of 13-column accounting paper, available at any office supply store. Label one page "cash receipts journal" and another "cash disbursements journal."

Let's say you want to record your recent sales using a manual system. In your cash receipts journal, label the columns to match the types of sales you have in your business (see table 17).

Label the columns with the date, who the money came from, the invoice number being paid, and the amount of payment. Then add a few columns for a specific business use. In this example, the small business owner fixes cars, so she wants to break out income into these categories—supplies, parts, labor, and miscellaneous.

There is no right or wrong way to categorize your sales—it's absolutely up to you. You may want to lump together all the *types* of income and break it out by *location* instead. It all depends on how you want to see your income patterns.

You will also use your cash receipts journal for any miscellaneous income to your business. You may have an interest-bearing checking account. If so, the interest income would be posted into your cash receipts journal.

If you made that journal entry like accountants do, it would look like this:

| CASH | $10 |
| INTEREST INCOME | $10 |

Recording the receipt of interest on checking account

SAMPLE COMPANY	CASH RECEIPTS JOURNAL						
DATE	FROM	INVOICE#	AMOUNT	SUPPLIES	PARTS	LABOR	MISC
1/4/20	SALLY ROGERS	459625841	$267.21	$42.71	$126.50	$93.00	$5.00
1/6/20	BUDDY SORRELL	459625877	$459.66	$46.20	$263.46	$145.00	$5.00
1/9/20	ROBERT PETRIE	459684255	$731.26	$54.00	$322.26	$350.00	$5.00
1/22/20	ALAN BRADY	459692245	$365.44	$46.00	$164.44	$150.00	$5.00
	TOTALS		$1,823.57	$188.91	$876.66	$738.00	$20.00

Table 17. Sample cash receipts journal

SAMPLE COMPANY CASH DISBURSEMENTS JOURNAL									
1252	1/1/20	XYZ OFFICE SUPPLY	PAPER	$25.49	$25.49				
1253	1/5/20	SA PROPERTY MGMT	RENT	$1,500.00		$1,500.00			
1254	1/7/20	NEEDA PHONE CO	PHONE SERVICE	$67.84			67.84		
1255	1/9/20	BRIGHT ELECTRIC	ELECTRIC	$125.88			125.88		
1256	1/22/20	AB INSURANCE CO	INSURANCE	$450.00				$450.00	INSURANCE
	JAN 20	TOTALS		$2,169.21	$25.49	$1,500.00	$193.72	$450.00	

Table 18. Sample cash disbursement journal

Next, on the sheet marked "cash disbursements journal," fill in the columns to match your business expenses.

It should look something like this (see table 18).

The information we're trying to capture in this accounting journal is the date, amount, and purpose of each cash disbursement, be it a check or an automatic transaction through your bank.

In table 18, take a look at the columns. You need columns for for the check number, the date, the name and description, and the amount. Then there are columns for expenses you incur frequently, such as supplies, rent, and utilities. At the end of the sheet, label the next-to-last column "other," and use it for any expense or disbursement you don't have a column for. Use the last column to put in a description.

Use one page a month. List each business transaction as it happens, and keep all deposit slips, receipts, check stubs, and so on in a file folder or large envelope for that month. That way you will have something to back up each transaction. This is important at tax time (both because it makes doing taxes easier, and it minimizes chances of being audited). Keep these journals and file folders or envelopes for three to seven years.

Every time you make a deposit or receive cash, write it down in your cash receipts journal. Every time you spend money for the business, write it down in your cash disbursements journal. Then, at month's end, total up all your columns, and you'll have all your sales and expenses for the month.

That's a simplified version of a manual bookkeeping system. When your business grows, or if you feel more comfortable using a computerized system, then you can think about using a software program instead of a spreadsheet to record your transactions. Computerized accounting programs are made to do all the posting of journal entries for you. All you have to do is enter a check or record a deposit. The software does the rest.

One last task of business setup is creating a filing system. You should get a file cabinet or box, and organize it with files for your bills to pay, invoices owed to you, receipts, expenses paid, and so forth. Your system should make organizational sense to you and kept current.

You should also keep a reference file for all contracts, employee paperwork, receipts for assets purchased, lease contracts, customer information, and vendor information. Keep these files for as long as you're in business.

Then, set up a file for accounting records and keep all receipts, sales invoices, bank statements, credit card statements, bills paid, and tax returns. Keep these records together by year, and keep them for seven years.

BALANCE SHEET	
ASSETS:	
CASH IN CHECKING	$5,500
TOTAL ASSETS	$5,500
LIABILITIES:	
NONE	$0
EQUITY:	
COMMON STOCK	$1,000
PREFERRED STOCK	$4,500
TOTAL LIABILITIES & EQUITY	$5,500

Table 19. Initial issuance of stock on the Balance Sheet

STOCK

If you're the owner of a corporation, you will be purchasing shares of stock from it. Two classes of stock are used in small businesses: common and preferred. Common stock is used more than preferred stock. Common stock's value appreciates as the business's value grows, and the owners of common stock get voting rights and dividends. Preferred stock's value doesn't change, but its owners get preference in receiving dividends. And if the business fails, the owners of preferred stock get preference in receiving their investment back over common stock owners.

Large corporations listed on the stock exchange have many investor-owners and keep watch over their stock values all the time. Small companies, however, usually only have one or maybe a handful of owners, and the issuance of stock is merely the initial investment of cash into the business.

Stock is issued "at par," or at face value. If stock sells for less than the face value, it's considered "under par." Large corporations may issue (sell) thousands of stocks to bring money into the corporation. These stocks will be issued at various stated values, but many companies issue stock at low par values, say of $1.00 or less.

Most small corporations with one owner will issue the owner 500 shares of $1.00 par common stock. The owner will pay $500 for the stock, which starts the company with some operating cash, and the owner officially has a net worth of $500.

The journal entry for this transaction would look like this:

DEBIT: CASH	$500
CREDIT: COMMON STOCK	$500

If the company were to have multiple owners, and issue both common and preferred stock, you would see a journal entry more like this:

DEBIT: CASH	$5,500
CREDIT: COMMON STOCK	$1,000
CREDIT: PREFERRED STOCK	$4,500

This would reflect the issuance of 100 shares of $10 par common stock, and the issuance of 300 shares of $15 par preferred stock.

This transaction will show on your balance sheet, as seen in table 19. It will affect the asset and equity section by increasing your balance in your cash account and in your common stock account.

As with all balance sheets, notice that the total assets equal the total of all liabilities and equity accounts.

SETTING UP PAYROLL

Many small businesses start with just one owner and no employees, but if you're starting a restaurant, for example, you will need some help. Hiring employees and setting up payroll is not something to be taken lightly. In fact, you will need to be aware of, and adhere to, many laws and regulations.

You should have application forms, employee review forms, and so on. Keep employee records in a safe place, preferably a locking file cabinet. Keep them for 10 years, or as long as you're in business.

First, check out the Department of Labor website and your state website for minimum wage laws and overtime regulations. You will also need an I-9 Form for each employee to prove that he or she is legally able to work in the United States.

Next, go to the IRS website and apply for an Employer Identification Number (EIN). This is the number that will identify your business to the IRS as an employer and taxpayer.

Finally, go to the website for EFTPS, or Electronic Federal Taxpayer Payment System. Here you will sign up to make your payroll tax payments online. You will find the rules for payments on the IRS website. Basically, you have to pay the employer taxes either every time you pay your employees (semi-monthly payer) or each month (monthly payer). It depends on the level of employment taxes you'll be paying. Usually anything over $50,000 in six months makes you a semi-monthly depositor.

There are many options for payroll—you can calculate it yourself using the tax tables available online from the federal and state tax departments, or you can outsource it to one of the many available payroll firms like Paychex or ADP.

Here are all the types of employer taxes:

- *Federal Withholding Taxes*
  These are taxes withheld from the employee's wages and paid to the IRS based on the employee's wage. You'll use tax tables that list amounts due based on the wage amount, the employee's marital status, and the employee's number of exemptions (dependents).
- *Social Security and Medicare Taxes*
  These taxes are both paid to the IRS, but they are typically calculated separately. Social Security is calculated at 6.2 percent of the employee's taxable wages. Medicare is calculated at 1.45 percent. There are limits on these taxes, and they change every year, so check the IRS website each year to keep current. These

taxes are withheld from the employee's wages, plus paid by you, the employer (and so is considered a "fringe benefit" for employees). The total is then remitted to the IRS.

- *State Withholding Taxes*
  You can find information on your state withholding tax on your state's website. Some states collect school district taxes as well. Look for the Department of Taxation, and search for Employment Taxes to find the tax tables for your state. You will need to file paperwork with your state tax department to submit and pay employment taxes for your employees.

- *Local Withholding Taxes*
  The city or town in which your business operates will usually have a tax that you will have to withhold from your employees' paychecks and pay to the locality for them. Your employees may also live in a different locality that requires them to pay a local tax on their wages. You can withhold and pay that tax for them if you choose. Go to your city website and search for employment taxes, or business taxes, and look for withholding taxes. You will need to apply to withhold and pay local withholding taxes as well.

There are also employment taxes that are not withheld from the employee's wages, but rather are paid by you, the employer.

- *Federal Unemployment Tax*
  This tax is calculated quarterly, and needs to be paid to the IRS when the amount reaches $500. Right now the tax is paid for each employee up to $7,000 in wages. Go to the IRS website for details.

- *State Unemployment Tax*
  This tax is calculated and paid quarterly to your state taxation department. It is paid on each employee's wages up to a certain amount, depending on your state.

- *Workers' Compensation Insurance*
  This isn't really a tax but an insurance fund that employers pay to cover injuries to employees at work. Some states allow a business to self-insure. Employers pay a certain percentage of each employee's wages, depending on the job. Check your state website for more information.

Then there are other fringe benefits or withholdings for your employees, such as child support payments, garnishments, health savings account deposits, and medical premium payments.

BALANCE SHEET AS OF MARCH 31, 2020		CHANGE	NEW BALANCE
CASH IN CHECKING	$5,600	**(A)** -$140 **(B)** -$400	$5,460 $5,060
ACCOUNTS RECEIVABLE	$25,000		
INVENTORY	$4,500		
PREPAID INSURANCE & TAXES	$4,300		
UNEARNED REVENUE	$800		
PLANT ASSETS	$234,800		
LESS ACCUMULATED DEPRECIATION	$-20,000		
TOTAL ASSETS	$255,000		
ACCOUNTS PAYABLE	$2,800		
SALES TAX PAYABLE	$1,200		
PAYROLL TAXES PAYABLE	$6,000	**(A)** $140	$6,140
CREDIT CARD PAYABLE	$1,500		
LOAN PAYABLE	$5,000		
NOTE PAYABLE OWNER	$205,000		
TOTAL LIABILITIES	$222,300		
COMMON STOCK	$500		
PREFERRED STOCK	$2,200		
RETAINED EARNINGS	$60,000		
DIVIDENDS	$-30,000		
TOTAL EQUITY	$32,700		
TOTAL LIABILITIES & EQUITY	$255,000		
INCOME STATEMENT MONTH ENDED MARCH 31, 2020			
SALES	$300,000		
SALES RETURNS	$-15,000		
INTEREST INCOME	$100		
TOTAL REVENUE	$285,100		
COST OF GOODS SOLD	$148,500		
GROSS MARGIN	$136,600		
ADVERTISING EXPENSE	$6,500		
RENT EXPENSE	$3,800		
FEDERAL INCOME TAX	$600		
INSURANCE EXPENSE	$3,500		
UTILITIES EXPENSE	$6,000		
DUES & SUBSCRIPTIONS	$2,000		
GROSS WAGES	$78,000		
PAYROLL TAXES AND BENEFITS	$13,155	**(B)** $400	$13,555
INTEREST EXPENSE	$6,000		
BAD DEBT EXPENSE	$2,000		
DEPRECIATION EXPENSE	$6,000		
TOTAL EXPENSES	$127,555		
PROFIT/LOSS	$9,045		

EMPLOYEE BENEFITS AND TAXES

Once you have employees, or if you're paying yourself as an employee (as in an S corporation), you'll want to determine what employee benefits your company can afford to offer. These may include any or all of the following:

- Medical insurance
- Dental insurance
- 401(k) retirement plans
- Health savings accounts
- Group life insurance
- Disability insurance

With these benefits, if the employee pays a portion of the cost, you would deduct that portion from the employee's wages. When you post your payroll, you would post that portion to a liability account, such as "401(k) withholding payable." Then when you write a check to your 401(k) plan provider, you would post a cash disbursement to reduce the payable.

DEBIT: PAYROLL TAXES PAYABLE	$140
CREDIT: CASH IN CHECKING	$140

This would show up on your Balance Sheet in the Liabilities section. See note **(A)**. For simplicity, we've used a summary account called "Payroll Taxes Payable."

If the company pays the entire cost of the benefit, you would pay the cost of the benefit and post it as an expense.

DEBIT: PAYROLL TAXES AND BENEFITS	$400
CREDIT: CASH IN CHECKING	$400

This will be shown on your Income Statement as an expense, see note **(B)**. Here, again for simplicity, we've called the expense account "Payroll Taxes and Benefits."

BALANCE SHEET AS OF MARCH 31, 2020		CHANGE	NEW BALANCE
CASH IN CHECKING	$5,600	(A) -$169.35	$5,430.65
ACCOUNTS RECEIVABLE	$25,000		
INVENTORY	$4,500		
PREPAID INSURANCE & TAXES	$4,300		
UNEARNED REVENUE	$800		
PLANT ASSETS	$234,800		
LESS ACCUMULATED DEPRECIATION	$-20,000		
TOTAL ASSETS	$255,000		
ACCOUNTS PAYABLE	$2,800		
SALES TAX PAYABLE	$1,200		
PAYROLL TAXES PAYABLE	$6,000	(A) -$30.65 (B) - $15.30	$5,969.35 $5,954.05
CREDIT CARD PAYABLE	$1,500		
LOAN PAYABLE	$5,000		
NOTE PAYABLE OWNER	$205,000		
TOTAL LIABILITIES	$222,300		
COMMON STOCK	$500		
PREFERRED STOCK	$2,200		
RETAINED EARNINGS	$60,000		
DIVIDENDS	$-30,000		
TOTAL EQUITY	$32,700		
TOTAL LIABILITIES & EQUITY	$255,000		
INCOME STATEMENT MONTH ENDED MARCH 31, 2020			
SALES	$300,000		
SALES RETURNS	$-15,000		
INTEREST INCOME	$100		
TOTAL REVENUE	$285,100		
COST OF GOODS SOLD	$148,500		
GROSS MARGIN	$136,600		
ADVERTISING EXPENSE	$6,500		
RENT EXPENSE	$3,800		
FEDERAL INCOME TAX	$600		
INSURANCE EXPENSE	$3,500		
UTILITIES EXPENSE	$6,000		
DUES & SUBSCRIPTIONS	$2,000		
GROSS WAGES	$78,000	(A) $200.00	$78,200.00
PAYROLL TAXES AND BENEFITS	$13,155	(B) $15.30	$13,170.30
INTEREST EXPENSE	$6,000		
BAD DEBT EXPENSE	$2,000		
DEPRECIATION EXPENSE	$6,000		
TOTAL EXPENSES	$127,555		
PROFIT/LOSS	$9,045		

Posting Payroll and Taxes

When you pay employees, you withhold the taxes and any other deductions from their gross wages and then pay that money to the tax department or governing body for that deduction.

Let's say you have one part-time employee, and you pay her weekly:

GROSS WAGES	$200.00	
FICA	- 12.40	($200 X 6.2 PERCENT)
MEDICARE	- 2.90	($200 X 1.45 PERCENT)
FEDERAL WITHHOLDING	- 11.00	PER TAX TABLE
STATE WITHHOLDING	- 1.35	PER TAX TABLE
LOCAL WITHHOLDING	- 3.00	($200 X 1.5 PERCENT)
NET PAY	169.35	

FICA tax, Medicare tax, and federal withholding tax are all posted to the same liability account since they are all paid to the IRS.

The paycheck above would be posted in a journal entry as:

DEBIT: GROSS WAGES EXPENSE	$200.00
CREDIT: FICA/FEDERAL WITHHOLDING PAYABLE	$26.30
CREDIT: STATE WITHHOLDING PAYABLE	$1.35
CREDIT: LOCAL WITHHOLDING PAYABLE	$3.00
CREDIT: CASH IN CHECKING	$169.35

Gross wages is an expense and will show on your Income Statement. The employer portion (not the employee portion) of the FICA taxes will also show on your Income Statement under expenses. See note **(A)**.

FICA and Medicare are the taxes that both the employee and the employer pays, so you would make an additional journal entry for the above payroll like this:

DEBIT: FICA EXPENSE	$15.30
CREDIT: FICA/FEDERAL WITHHOLDING PAYABLE	$15.30

Deductions that you have withheld, but not yet paid, are liabilities and will show in that section of your balance sheet. The FICA Expense will be on your Income Statement as an expense. See note **(B)**.

BALANCE SHEET AS OF MARCH 31, 2020		CHANGE	NEW BALANCE
CASH IN CHECKING	$5,600	(A) -$41.60 (B) -$300.00	$5,558.40 $5,258.40
ACCOUNTS RECEIVABLE	$25,000		
INVENTORY	$4,500		
PREPAID INSURANCE & TAXES	$4,300		
UNEARNED REVENUE	$800		
PLANT ASSETS	$234,800		
LESS ACCUMULATED DEPRECIATION	$-20,000		
TOTAL ASSETS	$255,000		
ACCOUNTS PAYABLE	$2,800		
SALES TAX PAYABLE	$1,200		
PAYROLL TAXES PAYABLE	$6,000	(A) - $41.60	$5,958.40
CREDIT CARD PAYABLE	$1,500		
LOAN PAYABLE	$5,000		
NOTE PAYABLE OWNER	$205,000		
TOTAL LIABILITIES	$222,300		
COMMON STOCK	$500		
PREFERRED STOCK	$2,200		
RETAINED EARNINGS	$60,000		
DIVIDENDS	$-30,000		
TOTAL EQUITY	$32,700		
TOTAL LIABILITIES & EQUITY	$255,000		
INCOME STATEMENT MONTH ENDED MARCH 31, 2020			
SALES	$300,000		
SALES RETURNS	$-15,000		
INTEREST INCOME	$100		
TOTAL REVENUE	$285,100		
COST OF GOODS SOLD	$148,500		
GROSS MARGIN	$136,600		
ADVERTISING EXPENSE	$6,500		
RENT EXPENSE	$3,800		
FEDERAL INCOME TAX	$600		
INSURANCE EXPENSE	$3,500		
UTILITIES EXPENSE	$6,000		
DUES & SUBSCRIPTIONS	$2,000		
GROSS WAGES	$78,000		
PAYROLL TAXES AND BENEFITS	$13,155	(B) $300.00	$13,455.00
INTEREST EXPENSE	$6,000		
BAD DEBT EXPENSE	$2,000		
DEPRECIATION EXPENSE	$6,000		
TOTAL EXPENSES	$127,555		
PROFIT/LOSS	$9,045		

Paying Employment Taxes

When you pay those tax liabilities, you would write a check to the taxing authority and post a disbursement like this:

DEBIT: FICA/FEDERAL
    WITHHOLDING PAYABLE $41.60
CREDIT: CASH IN CHECKING $41.60

See note **(A)**.

When you pay the employer-only taxes, such as unemployment, those are posted as expenses:

DEBIT: STATE UNEMPLOYMENT
    TAX EXPENSE $300
CREDIT: CASH IN CHECKING $300

See note **(B)**.

State unemployment taxes are reported and paid quarterly, and workers' compensation is usually paid biannually. Federal unemployment taxes are calculated quarterly and paid once the total reaches $500. The tax return (Form 940) is filed at year-end. FICA and federal withholding taxes are either paid with each payroll or paid once a month. That tax return (Form 941) is filed quarterly. State withholding and local withholding taxes have returns also, and those are filed and paid quarterly. Refer to the beginning of this chapter for detailed information on how/where to pay each tax.

BALANCE SHEET AS OF MARCH 31, 2020		CHANGE	NEW BALANCE
CASH IN CHECKING	$5,600	(C) $-780	$4,620
ACCOUNTS RECEIVABLE	$25,000		
INVENTORY	$4,500		
PREPAID INSURANCE & TAXES	$4,300		
UNEARNED REVENUE	$800		
PLANT ASSETS	$234,800	(A) $750	$235,550
LESS ACCUM DEPRECIATION	$-20,000		
TOTAL ASSETS	$255,000		
ACCOUNTS PAYABLE	$2,800		
SALES TAX PAYABLE	$1,200		
PAYROLL TAXES PAYABLE	$6,000		
CREDIT CARD PAYABLE	$1,500	(A) $750 (B) $30 (C) - $780	$2,250 $2,280 $1,500
LOAN PAYABLE	$5,000		
NOTE PAYABLE OWNER	$205,000		
TOTAL LIABILITIES	$222,300		
COMMON STOCK	$500		
PREFERRED STOCK	$2,200		
RETAINED EARNINGS	$60,000		
DIVIDENDS	$-30,000		
TOTAL EQUITY	$32,700		
TOTAL LIABILITIES & EQUITY	$255,000		
INCOME STATEMENT MONTH ENDED MARCH 31, 2020			
SALES	$300,000		
SALES RETURNS	$-15,000		
INTEREST INCOME	$100		
TOTAL REVENUE	$285,100		
COST OF GOODS SOLD	$148,500		
GROSS MARGIN	$136,600		
ADVERTISING EXPENSE	$6,500		
RENT EXPENSE	$3,800		
FEDERAL INCOME TAX	$600		
INSURANCE EXPENSE	$3,500		
UTILITIES EXPENSE	$6,000		
DUES & SUBSCRIPTIONS	$2,000		
GROSS WAGES	$78,000		
PAYROLL TAXES AND BENEFITS	$13,155		
INTEREST EXPENSE	$6,000	(B) $30	$6,030
BAD DEBT EXPENSE	$2,000		
DEPRECIATION EXPENSE	$6,000		
TOTAL EXPENSES	$127,555		
PROFIT/LOSS	$9,045		

BORROWING

Most small businesses at some time will need to borrow money, whether from the owner, a bank, or even from a friend or family member. When just starting out, it's very hard to borrow money from a bank. You will want to be in business for at least two years before you try going to a bank for a loan.

But there are other means of borrowing, from family to credit cards to 401(k) loans. When borrowing from friends or family, and even from yourself, be sure to create a legal promissory note that states the amount borrowed, any interest that will be paid, and the date the amount will be repaid. File this with your important business papers.

Sometimes small business owners use a credit card for expenses or even equipment purchases. This is a form of borrowing, since you will be paying interest to the credit card company if you can't pay the card off each month. This is handled a little differently than borrowing from a bank.

When you buy something on a business credit card, you should post the purchase and the amount due to the credit card company:

DEBIT: OFFICE EQUIPMENT	$750
CREDIT: CREDIT CARD PAYABLE	$750

This entry books your asset (office equipment) and your liability (credit card payable) for this transaction. See note **(A)**.

At the end of the month, you get your credit card statement. Let's suppose you weren't able to pay the amount in full, and they've charged you interest. You would then incur interest expense and an increase in the credit card payable (the amount you owe).

DEBIT: INTEREST EXPENSE	$30
CREDIT: CREDIT CARD PAYABLE	$30

This entry books the interest and the additional amount due to the credit card company. These accounts will show on your Income Statement under Interest Expense: note **(B)**.

Then the next month, when you pay the bill, you will post a disbursement to the liability account like this:

DEBIT: CREDIT CARD PAYABLE	$780
CREDIT: CASH IN CHECKING	$780

See note **(C)**.

Once you've been in business for a few years, you can try to borrow from a bank for cash-flow purposes, or to help cover growth or expansion costs. You will need to

BALANCE SHEET AS OF MARCH 31, 2020		CHANGE	NEW BALANCE
CASH IN CHECKING	$5,600	(A) $5,000.00 (B) -$434.94	$10,165.06
ACCOUNTS RECEIVABLE	$25,000		
INVENTORY	$4,500		
PREPAID INSURANCE & TAXES	$4,300		
UNEARNED REVENUE	$800		
PLANT ASSETS	$234,800		
LESS ACCUM DEPRECIATION	$-20,000		
TOTAL ASSETS	$255,000		
ACCOUNTS PAYABLE	$2,800		
SALES TAX PAYABLE	$1,200		
PAYROLL TAXES PAYABLE	$6,000		
CREDIT CARD PAYABLE	$1,500		
LOAN PAYABLE	$5,000	(A) $5,000.00 (B) -$401.61	$9,598.39
NOTE PAYABLE OWNER	$205,000		
TOTAL LIABILITIES	$222,300		
COMMON STOCK	$500		
PREFERRED STOCK	$2,200		
RETAINED EARNINGS	$60,000		
DIVIDENDS	$-30,000		
TOTAL EQUITY	$32,700		
TOTAL LIABILITIES & EQUITY	$255,000		
INCOME STATEMENT MONTH ENDED MARCH 31, 2020			
SALES	$300,000		
SALES RETURNS	$-15,000		
INTEREST INCOME	$100		
TOTAL REVENUE	$285,100		
COST OF GOODS SOLD	$148,500		
GROSS MARGIN	$136,600		
ADVERTISING EXPENSE	$6,500		
RENT EXPENSE	$3,800		
FEDERAL INCOME TAX	$600		
INSURANCE EXPENSE	$3,500		
UTILITIES EXPENSE	$6,000		
DUES & SUBSCRIPTIONS	$2,000		
GROSS WAGES	$78,000		
PAYROLL TAXES AND BENEFITS	$13,155		
INTEREST EXPENSE	$6,000	$33.33	$6,033.33
BAD DEBT EXPENSE	$2,000		
DEPRECIATION EXPENSE	$6,000		
TOTAL EXPENSES	$127,555		
PROFIT/LOSS	$9,045		

provide the bank with two or three years of financial statements, and usually a cash flow projection for the coming year. The bank wants to be confident that it's going to be paid back.

Borrowing to purchase a building, equipment, or a vehicle is usually easier because the bank will have collateral to take back if you can't make the payments. You will probably need to sign a personal guarantee as well. Make it a habit to check your personal credit at least yearly, and to establish some business credit as well. Good credit will make borrowing much easier.

How Do You Get Business Credit?

Set up a few vendor accounts when you can. That means the vendor will allow you to purchase on credit and will send you a bill to pay, rather than make you pay upon purchase. Then get a business credit card and pay it promptly. This will help build business credit. Always try to keep your personal credit clean as well, and make all payments on time—your personal credit will be just as important as your business credit, at least until the business establishes several years of credit on its own.

Bank Borrowing

When you borrow money from a bank, you will receive a lump sum, which you will deposit into your bank account.

DEBIT: CASH IN CHECKING $5,000
CREDIT: VEHICLE LOAN PAYABLE $5,000

The loan account will show on your Balance Sheet under Liabilities. See note **(A)**.

You will then make payments to the bank each month. These payments will be part principal (loan amount) and part interest.

When you make that first month's payment, you would post a disbursement like this, see note **(B)**.

DEBIT: VEHICLE LOAN PAYABLE $401.61
DEBIT: INTEREST EXPENSE $33.33
CREDIT: CASH IN CHECKING $434.94

That disbursement would post the total amount paid, which is broken down into principal and interest. The principal portion is not an expense; it is what is called a "balance sheet item," and it reduces the liability. The interest portion, however, is an expense and will show up on your income statement. See note **(B)**.

Simple interest is calculated based on the amount borrowed, the rate of interest, and the number of months the amount is borrowed for.

3

////////////

RUNNING A BUSINESS

Once your business is up and running, you'll need to keep track of many transactions. You'll need to track all costs associated with your business, including direct costs and indirect costs.

Direct costs are costs directly associated with producing your product or providing your service.

Indirect costs (also called overhead) are costs needed to operate the business, but are not directly involved in making the product or providing the service. These would be things like rent, electricity, phone and Internet service, administrative employee wages, advertising costs, accountant fees, IT services, attorney fees, and business insurance. These costs need to be paid regardless of whether you make any widgets. Do the research so you have a general sense of what your costs will be.

Next up is buying the essential equipment for your company. Once you do that (and have a place to do business), then you can finally start operations.

BALANCE SHEET AS OF MARCH 31, 2020		CHANGE	NEW BALANCE
CASH IN CHECKING	$5,600	**(A)** -$3,704	$1,896
ACCOUNTS RECEIVABLE	$25,000		
INVENTORY	$4,500		
PREPAID INSURANCE & TAXES	$4,300		
UNEARNED REVENUE	$800		
PLANT ASSETS	$234,800	**(A)** $3,704 **(B)** $3,000	$238,504
LESS ACCUM DEPRECIATION	$-20,000		
TOTAL ASSETS	$255,000		
ACCOUNTS PAYABLE	$2,800		
SALES TAX PAYABLE	$1,200		
PAYROLL TAXES PAYABLE	$6,000		
CREDIT CARD PAYABLE	$1,500	**(B)** $3,000	
LOAN PAYABLE	$5,000		
NOTE PAYABLE OWNER	$205,000		
TOTAL LIABILITIES	$222,300		
COMMON STOCK	$500		
PREFERRED STOCK	$2,200		
RETAINED EARNINGS	$60,000		
DIVIDENDS	$-30,000		
TOTAL EQUITY	$32,700		
TOTAL LIABILITIES & EQUITY	$255,000		
INCOME STATEMENT MONTH ENDED MARCH 31, 2020			
SALES	$300,000		
SALES RETURNS	$-15,000		
INTEREST INCOME	$100		
TOTAL REVENUE	$285,100		
COST OF GOODS SOLD	$148,500		
GROSS MARGIN	$136,600		
ADVERTISING EXPENSE	$6,500		
RENT EXPENSE	$3,800		
FEDERAL INCOME TAX	$600		
INSURANCE EXPENSE	$3,500		
UTILITIES EXPENSE	$6,000		
DUES & SUBSCRIPTIONS	$2,000		
GROSS WAGES	$78,000		
PAYROLL TAXES AND BENEFITS	$13,155		
INTEREST EXPENSE	$6,000		
BAD DEBT EXPENSE	$2,000		
DEPRECIATION EXPENSE	$6,000		
TOTAL EXPENSES	$127,555		
PROFIT/LOSS	$9,045		

ORDERING EQUIPMENT

When you set up your business, you may need equipment to get started. You may need lawn mowers and leaf blowers, or you may need kitchen equipment, or you may need table saws and other power tools. Whatever the specific equipment needs of your business, you will need to keep track of those assets.

Property, plant, and equipment is a specific asset class on your balance sheet and includes buildings, building improvements, and equipment used in your business.

When you buy equipment, you have just purchased an asset. But what is considered the real cost of that asset? The cost of an asset includes the purchase price of the asset, plus any costs associated with getting it to you and ready to use. So if you are starting a restaurant, you may need to buy a chef's stove and an industrial refrigerator. You will need to have it delivered and set into place in your restaurant. Here's the cost of your equipment purchase:

INDUSTRIAL STOVE	$1,500
INDUSTRIAL FRIDGE	$1,800
SALES TAX	$54
DELIVERY AND SETUP	$350
TOTAL COST	$3,704

Here's the journal entry you would make:

KITCHEN EQUIPMENT	$3,704
CASH	$3,704

Recording the purchase of an industrial stove and refrigerator for the business.

These assets would show up on your Balance Sheet. See note **(A)**.

If you are starting up a lawn care business, you would need at least a mower, a trimmer, and a trailer to haul your equipment from job to job.

Here's the journal entry you would make:

LAWN CARE EQUIPMENT	$1,700
TRAILER	$1,300
CASH	$3,000

Recording purchase of a mower, a trimmer, and a trailer for the business.

Asset accounts, like equipment or vehicles, show on your Balance Sheet as in note **(B)**.

BALANCE SHEET AS OF MARCH 31, 2020		CHANGE	NEW BALANCE
CASH IN CHECKING	$5,600		
ACCOUNTS RECEIVABLE	$25,000		
INVENTORY	$4,500		
PREPAID INSURANCE & TAXES	$4,300		
UNEARNED REVENUE	$800		
LAND	$0	(C) $5,000	$5,000
PLANT ASSETS	$234,800	(C) $15,000	$249,800
LESS ACCUMDEPRECIATION	$-20,000		
TOTAL ASSETS	$255,000		
ACCOUNTS PAYABLE	$2,800		
SALES TAX PAYABLE	$1,200		
PAYROLL TAXES PAYABLE	$6,000		
CREDIT CARD PAYABLE	$1,500		
LOAN PAYABLE	$5,000		
NOTE PAYABLE OWNER	$205,000	(C) $20,000	$225,000
TOTAL LIABILITIES	$222,300		
COMMON STOCK	$500		
PREFERRED STOCK	$2,200		
RETAINED EARNINGS	$60,000		
DIVIDENDS	$-30,000		
TOTAL EQUITY	**$32,700**		
TOTAL LIABILITIES & EQUITY	**$255,000**		
INCOME STATEMENT MONTH ENDED MARCH 31, 2020			
SALES	$300,000		
SALES RETURNS	$-15,000		
INTEREST INCOME	$100		
TOTAL REVENUE	$285,100		
COST OF GOODS SOLD	$148,500		
GROSS MARGIN	$136,600		
ADVERTISING EXPENSE	$6,500		
RENT EXPENSE	$3,800		
FEDERAL INCOME TAX	$600		
INSURANCE EXPENSE	$3,500		
UTILITIES EXPENSE	$6,000		
DUES & SUBSCRIPTIONS	$2,000		
GROSS WAGES	$78,000		
PAYROLL TAXES AND BENEFITS	$13,155		
INTEREST EXPENSE	$6,000		
BAD DEBT EXPENSE	$2,000		
DEPRECIATION EXPENSE	$6,000		
TOTAL EXPENSES	**$127,555**		
PROFIT/LOSS	**$9,045**		

If you are starting a doggie day care, you will need a place to keep the dogs. So, let's say you purchase a piece of property with a house, an outbuilding, and a fenced-in area for the dogs. You take out a mortgage of $180,000, with $145,000 designated for the house, $15,000 for the outbuilding, and $20,000 for the land. Of that, $15,000 is for the house and yard, and $5,000 is for the land with the outbuilding and fenced-in area.

The house is personal property. The outbuilding and fenced-in area will be business property. So the mortgage is not a business loan since you will owe the mortgage personally. You will then technically lend the company the amount allocated to the outbuilding and land, which will be the business assets. So the business now owes you $20,000 and should make payments to you each month.

Here's what the balance sheet for the doggie day care would look like at the end of the month (see the balance sheet).

Assets are listed on one side, and liabilities and equity on the other (remember the accounting equation).

The journal entry for the business assets is:

LAND	$5,000
BUILDING AND IMPROVEMENTS	$15,000
NOTE PAYABLE–OWNER	$20,000

Recording purchase of land and building for the business, and loan amount due owner.

Land and building are shown in the example Balance Sheet under a summary account "Plant Assets." The Note Payable account is listed in the Liability section. See note **(C)**.

Once you have your property and equipment in place, you're ready for business.

ASSETS:		LIABILITIES:	
CASH	$4,000	NOTE PAYABLE–PROPERTY	$20,000
LAND	$5,000		
BUILDING	$15,000	EQUITY:	
		OWNER'S EQUITY	$4,000
TOTAL ASSETS	**$24,000**	**TOTAL LIAB. & EQUITY**	**$24,000**

Table 20.

BALANCE SHEET AS OF MARCH 31, 2020		CHANGE	NEW BALANCE
CASH IN CHECKING	$5,600		
ACCOUNTS RECEIVABLE	$25,000		
INVENTORY	$4,500	**(A)** $31.03 **(B)** -$31.03	$4,531.03 $4,500.00
PREPAID INSURANCE & TAXES	$4,300		
UNEARNED REVENUE	$800		
PLANT ASSETS	$234,800		
LESS ACCUM DEPRECIATION	$-20,000		
TOTAL ASSETS	$255,000		
ACCOUNTS PAYABLE	$2,800	**(A)** $31.03 **(B)** -$31.03	$2,831.03 $2,800.00
SALES TAX PAYABLE	$1,200		
PAYROLL TAXES PAYABLE	$6,000		
CREDIT CARD PAYABLE	$1,500		
LOAN PAYABLE	$5,000		
NOTE PAYABLE OWNER	$205,000		
TOTAL LIABILITIES	$222,300		
COMMON STOCK	$500		
PREFERRED STOCK	$2,200		
RETAINED EARNINGS	$60,000		
DIVIDENDS	$-30,000		
TOTAL EQUITY	$32,700		
TOTAL LIABILITIES & EQUITY	$255,000		
INCOME STATEMENT MONTH ENDED MARCH 31, 2020			
SALES	$300,000		
SALES RETURNS	$-15,000		
INTEREST INCOME	$100		
TOTAL REVENUE	$285,100		
COST OF GOODS SOLD	$148,500		
GROSS MARGIN	$136,600		
ADVERTISING EXPENSE	$6,500		
RENT EXPENSE	$3,800		
FEDERAL INCOME TAX	$600		
INSURANCE EXPENSE	$3,500		
UTILITIES EXPENSE	$6,000		
DUES & SUBSCRIPTIONS	$2,000		
GROSS WAGES	$78,000		
PAYROLL TAXES AND BENEFITS	$13,155		
INTEREST EXPENSE	$6,000		
BAD DEBT EXPENSE	$2,000		
DEPRECIATION EXPENSE	$6,000		
TOTAL EXPENSES	$127,555		
PROFIT/LOSS	$9,045		

ORDERING AND RECEIVING MATERIALS

When you order materials, you incur what's called an accounts payable, which is a liability account. That just means you owe somebody for that purchase. Instead of paying cash at the point of purchase, you agree to pay in 30 days. If you manufacture products, you will have different materials that go together to make that product. You will also have finished products on hand. These parts and products are called inventory. Inventory is an asset.

Let's go through an example: Sally manufactures birdhouses. She buys one-by-six lengths of lumber for her houses. She buys shingles for the roofs, and dowels for the birds to stand on to get into the house. She also purchases nails to put the pieces together, as well as metal to use as hangers. These are all parts of the finished product.

Sally calls the lumber yard and orders one six-foot length of one-by-six board for $5, one package of 12 shingles for $12, two twelve-foot lengths of dowel for $2, one box of 48 nails for $6, and four metal hangers for $4.

Her purchase comes to $29, plus sales tax of $2.03, for a grand total of $31.03. The journal entry would be:

INVENTORY	$31.03
ACCOUNTS PAYABLE	$31.03

Recording the purchase of inventory items on credit.

Both of these accounts are on the Balance Sheet. See note **(A)**.

Sally uses the materials to start building birdhouses. And in 30 days she pays the bill to the lumber yard.

ACCOUNTS PAYABLE	$31.03
CASH	$31.03

Recording the payment of the lumber yard bill.

These accounts will appear on your Balance Sheet, see note **(B)**.

BALANCE SHEET AS OF MARCH 31, 2020		CHANGE	NEW BALANCE
CASH IN CHECKING	$5,600		
ACCOUNTS RECEIVABLE	$25,000		
INVENTORY	$4,500		
PREPAID INSURANCE & TAXES	$4,300		
UNEARNED REVENUE	$800		
PLANT ASSETS	$234,800		
LESS ACCUMULATED DEPRECIATION	$-20,000		
TOTAL ASSETS	$255,000		
ACCOUNTS PAYABLE	$2,800		
SALES TAX PAYABLE	$1,200		
PAYROLL TAXES PAYABLE	$6,000		
CREDIT CARD PAYABLE	$1,500		
LOAN PAYABLE	$5,000		
NOTE PAYABLE OWNER	$205,000		
TOTAL LIABILITIES	$222,300		
COMMON STOCK	$500		
PREFERRED STOCK	$2,200		
RETAINED EARNINGS	$60,000		
DIVIDENDS	$-30,000		
TOTAL EQUITY	$32,700		
TOTAL LIABILITIES & EQUITY	$255,000		
INCOME STATEMENT MONTH ENDED MARCH 31, 2020			
SALES	$300,000		
SALES RETURNS	$-15,000		
INTEREST INCOME	$100		
TOTAL REVENUE	$285,100		
COST OF GOODS SOLD	$148,500		
GROSS MARGIN	$136,600		
ADVERTISING EXPENSE	$6,500		
RENT EXPENSE	$3,800		
FEDERAL INCOME TAX	$600		
INSURANCE EXPENSE	$3,500		
UTILITIES EXPENSE	$6,000		
DUES & SUBSCRIPTIONS	$2,000		
GROSS WAGES	$78,000		
PAYROLL TAXES AND BENEFITS	$13,155		
INTEREST EXPENSE	$6,000		
BAD DEBT EXPENSE	$2,000		
DEPRECIATION EXPENSE	$6,000		
TOTAL EXPENSES	$127,555		
PROFIT/LOSS	$9,045		

OVERSEEING PRODUCTION

As your company orders materials, and makes products to sell, other business transactions are going on that you need to watch and take care of. You may have employees to track hours for and pay, bills for materials and overhead, and inventories to manage.

As you make products (or provide a service) you may have employees helping you, or you may subcontract out the work.

If you have one or more employees, you will need to pay them—weekly, biweekly, semimonthly, or monthly. You will need to have time cards or some other way for them to track their hours. And you will need to calculate payroll (see the previous section on paying employees).

When you pay your employees, keep shop wages separate from management and administrative wages. Why? Because shop wages—wages for employees directly making products or providing services—should be included in your cost of goods sold, whereas management and administrative wages should be listed in your expenses.

Remember that on the Income Statement, the cost of goods sold section is in between the revenue section and the expenses section (see table 21).

Besides COGS, many other costs are associated with running a business.

REVENUE	$50,000
LESS COST OF GOODS SOLD	-$35,000
GROSS MARGIN	$15,000
LESS EXPENSES	-$10,000
PROFIT (LOSS)	$5,000

Table 21. Income statement detail showing COGS

BALANCE SHEET AS OF MARCH 31, 2020		CHANGE	NEW BALANCE
CASH IN CHECKING	$15,600	(A) -$4,000	$11,600
		(B) -$250	$11,350
		(C) -$300	$11,050
ACCOUNTS RECEIVABLE	$15,000		
INVENTORY	$4,500		
PREPAID INSURANCE & TAXES	$4,300		
UNEARNED REVENUE	$800		
PLANT ASSETS	$234,800		
LESS ACCUM DEPRECIATION	$-20,000		
TOTAL ASSETS	$255,000		
ACCOUNTS PAYABLE	$2,800		
SALES TAX PAYABLE	$1,200		
PAYROLL TAXES PAYABLE	$6,000		
CREDIT CARD PAYABLE	$1,500		
LOAN PAYABLE	$5,000		
NOTE PAYABLE OWNER	$205,000		
TOTAL LIABILITIES	$222,300		
COMMON STOCK	$500		
PREFERRED STOCK	$2,200		
RETAINED EARNINGS	$60,000		
DIVIDENDS	$-30,000		
TOTAL EQUITY	$32,700		
TOTAL LIABILITIES & EQUITY	$255,000		
INCOME STATEMENT MONTH ENDED MARCH 31, 2020			
SALES	$300,000		
SALES RETURNS	$-15,000		
INTEREST INCOME	$100		
TOTAL REVENUE	$285,100		
COST OF GOODS SOLD	$148,500		
GROSS MARGIN	$136,600		
ADVERTISING EXPENSE	$6,500		
RENT EXPENSE	$3,800		
FEDERAL INCOME TAX	$600		
INSURANCE EXPENSE	$3,500		
UTILITIES EXPENSE	$6,000	(C) $300	$6,300
DUES & SUBSCRIPTIONS	$2,000	(B) $250	$2,250
GROSS WAGES	$78,000		
PAYROLL TAXES AND BENEFITS	$13,155	(A) $4,000	$17,155
INTEREST EXPENSE	$6,000		
BAD DEBT EXPENSE	$2,000		
DEPRECIATION EXPENSE	$6,000		
TOTAL EXPENSES	$127,555		
PROFIT/LOSS	$9,045		

THE COSTS OF DOING BUSINESS

We looked at overhead costs earlier. That's the indirect costs of operating a business—the expenses of keeping the doors open and the lights on, paying wages for employees, advertising, insuring the property and the business, employee benefit costs, membership fees and subscriptions to trade publications or groups, travel costs to seminars or trade shows, and other expenses incurred in keeping your business a viable and growing operation.

When you incur these costs, either you pay them at the time or you pay them on time, usually in 30 days. When you pay them at the time, you have a cash disbursement.

EMPLOYEE HEALTH INSURANCE EXPENSE	$4,000
CASH	$4,000

Recording the costs of health insurance for employees **(A)**.

DUES & SUBSCRIPTIONS	$250
CASH	$250

Recording annual membership fees to Retail Shop Owners of New Mexico **(B)**.

UTILITIES	$300
CASH	$300

Recording payment of electric bill for the month **(C)**.

These expense accounts appear on your Income Statement. For simplicity, the Employee Health Insurance Expense has been placed into a summary account called "Payroll Taxes and Benefits." See notes **(A) (B)** and **(C)**.

If you don't pay these costs as soon as you get the bill, but wait until they are due (as stated on the invoice), then you incur an accounts payable (arrow in the table).

Posting your bills into a computerized accounting system, to pay later when due, is one way of dealing with accounts payable. The computer system can then display a report that will show you all the bills that are due, or due by a certain date.

If you're keeping books by hand, though, you will need to keep a keep a file folder for your bills. You could label one folder for each week in the month, and put the bill in the folder for the week it's due. At the beginning of each month, pay the bills in the corresponding folder.

You could also keep a running list of bills and their due dates, so at any time you will know how much you have outstanding in accounts payable (see table 22).

ACCOUNTS PAYABLE:			
MAPLE STREET REALTY CO.	RENT EXPENSE	DUE MAY 10	$1,500
MILL VALLEY ELECTRIC CO.	UTILITIES EXPENSE	DUE MAY 14	$310
RETAILERS OF MILL VALLEY	SUBSCRIPTIONS EXPENSE	DUE MAY 17	$50
MILL VALLEY NEWS	ADVERTISING EXPENSE	DUE MAY 20	$100
VERIZON	TELEPHONE EXPENSE	DUE MAY 22	$240
WESTFIELD INSURANCE	INSURANCE EXPENSE	DUE MAY 25	$600
TOTAL ACCOUNTS PAYABLE			$2,800

Table 22. Accounts payable detail

Another cost of doing business is depreciation, a noncash expense. Depreciation represents the devaluing of your assets as you use them. For instance, a piece of machinery may have a useful life of 10 years. If you pay $15,000 for the machine, each year, owing to wear and tear, it is worth less. To show this, on the income statement we list an expense account called depreciation expense, and on the balance sheet we have an asset account called accumulated depreciation.

The first year of depreciation is deducted from the cost of the asset, to bring the book value of the asset down to $13,500. This reflects the wear and tear on the machine and more closely approximates what it would be worth for if you chose to sell it. The depreciation of $1,500 is an expense as well.

Here's the journal entry:

DEPRECIATION EXPENSE $1,500
ACCUMULATED DEPRECIATION $1,500

Booking the first year depreciation on a machine.

Table 22 illustrates where accumulated depreciation shows on the balance sheet. On the Income Statement statement below, you will find depreciation expense shown in note **(B)**.

How do you calculate depreciation? The IRS has specific rules on depreciation of property. See IRS Publication 946, available on IRS.gov. There you will find classes of assets, useful lives, methods of depreciation, and depreciation schedules.

BALANCE SHEET AS OF MARCH 31, 2020		CHANGE	NEW BALANCE
CASH IN CHECKING	$5,600		
ACCOUNTS RECEIVABLE	$25,000		
INVENTORY	$4,500		
PREPAID INSURANCE & TAXES	$4,300		
UNEARNED REVENUE	$800		
PLANT ASSETS	$234,800		
LESS ACCUMULATED DEPRECIATION	$-20,000	(B) - $1,500	-$21,500
TOTAL ASSETS	$255,000		
ACCOUNTS PAYABLE	$2,800		
SALES TAX PAYABLE	$1,200		
PAYROLL TAXES PAYABLE	$6,000		
CREDIT CARD PAYABLE	$1,500		
LOAN PAYABLE	$5,000		
NOTE PAYABLE OWNER	$205,000		
TOTAL LIABILITIES	$222,300		
COMMON STOCK	$500		
PREFERRED STOCK	$2,200		
RETAINED EARNINGS	$60,000		
DIVIDENDS	$-30,000		
TOTAL EQUITY	$32,700		
TOTAL LIABILITIES & EQUITY	$255,000		
INCOME STATEMENT MONTH ENDED MARCH 31, 2020			
SALES	$300,000		
SALES RETURNS	$-15,000		
INTEREST INCOME	$100		
TOTAL REVENUE	$285,100		
COST OF GOODS SOLD	$148,500		
GROSS MARGIN	$136,600		
ADVERTISING EXPENSE	$6,500		
RENT EXPENSE	$3,800		
FEDERAL INCOME TAX	$600		
INSURANCE EXPENSE	$3,500		
UTILITIES EXPENSE	$6,000		
DUES & SUBSCRIPTIONS	$2,000		
GROSS WAGES	$78,000		
PAYROLL TAXES AND BENEFITS	$13,155		
INTEREST EXPENSE	$6,000		
BAD DEBT EXPENSE	$2,000		
DEPRECIATION EXPENSE	$6,000	(B) $1,500	$7,500
TOTAL EXPENSES	$127,555		
PROFIT/LOSS	$9,045		

BALANCE SHEET AS OF MARCH 31, 2020		CHANGE	NEW BALANCE
CASH IN CHECKING	$5,600		
ACCOUNTS RECEIVABLE	$25,000		
INVENTORY	$4,500	(A) -$6.95	$4,493.05
PREPAID INSURANCE & TAXES	$4,300		
UNEARNED REVENUE	$800		
PLANT ASSETS	$234,800		
LESS ACCUMULATED DEPRECIATION	$-20,000		
TOTAL ASSETS	$255,000		
ACCOUNTS PAYABLE	$2,800		
SALES TAX PAYABLE	$1,200		
PAYROLL TAXES PAYABLE	$6,000		
CREDIT CARD PAYABLE	$1,500		
LOAN PAYABLE	$5,000		
NOTE PAYABLE OWNER	$205,000		
TOTAL LIABILITIES	$222,300		
COMMON STOCK	$500		
PREFERRED STOCK	$2,200		
RETAINED EARNINGS	$60,000		
DIVIDENDS	$-30,000		
TOTAL EQUITY	$32,700		
TOTAL LIABILITIES & EQUITY	$255,000		
INCOME STATEMENT MONTH ENDED MARCH 31, 2020			
SALES	$300,000		
SALES RETURNS	$-15,000		
INTEREST INCOME	$100		
TOTAL REVENUE	$285,100		
COST OF GOODS SOLD	$148,500	(A) $6.95	$148,506.95
GROSS MARGIN	$136,600		
ADVERTISING EXPENSE	$6,500		
RENT EXPENSE	$3,800		
FEDERAL INCOME TAX	$600		
INSURANCE EXPENSE	$3,500		
UTILITIES EXPENSE	$6,000		
DUES & SUBSCRIPTIONS	$2,000		
GROSS WAGES	$78,000		
PAYROLL TAXES AND BENEFITS	$13,155		
INTEREST EXPENSE	$6,000		
BAD DEBT EXPENSE	$2,000		
DEPRECIATION EXPENSE	$6,000		
TOTAL EXPENSES	$127,555		
PROFIT/LOSS	$9,045		

INVENTORY AND COST OF GOODS SOLD

In the previous example of Sally building birdhouses, we went through the process of calculating the cost of an inventory item and the process of calculating the value of remaining inventory.

When Sally builds a birdhouse, she has used inventory items and should make a journal entry to transfer the cost of building the birdhouse from inventory to cost of goods sold (COGS).

Cost of goods sold is the account that keeps a running balance of the direct costs of manufacturing products. If you're selling services instead of manufacturing a product, you'll have an account called cost of sales, but it's the same concept. You post direct labor to your COGS account as well as freighting costs, subcontract costs, and any other cost of directly manufacturing the product.

Sally built a birdhouse for a cost of $6.95. She needs to take those material costs out of inventory and move them into COGS. So she makes the entry below, which increases the COGS account and decreases inventory, which is an asset account.

COST OF GOODS SOLD	$6.95
INVENTORY	$6.95

Transferring the cost of building one birdhouse to COGS.

Cost of goods sold can also have what are called "subaccounts." You can make COGS the summary account, and use subaccounts to track things like direct labor, materials, freight, and subcontract.

For the placement of cost of goods sold on an Income Statement, and inventory on the Balance Sheet, see note **(A)**.

4

//////////////////////

SELLING

N ow that your business is up and running, complete with equipment and inventory, the next step is to make a sale.

When you sell a product, you receive cash or a promise to pay. That promise to pay is called accounts receivable and is the opposite of accounts payable. When you have an accounts payable, you owe somebody, and when you have an accounts receivable, somebody owes you.

You need to track your accounts receivable, and make sure your customers pay on time. A computerized software accounting program will do this for you— all you need to do is prepare the invoice, mail it out, then monitor your accounts receivable balance.

If you're keeping a manual set of books, you need to make a list that includes invoice numbers/dates, payment due dates, and amounts. This is called an accounts receivable journal (see table 23).

You should also start a file for accounts receivable. You may want to include a sheet or file folder for each customer and list their specific invoices and related amounts and dates.

Give the customer 30 days to pay. Send out a reminder in 20 days, as a courtesy. If the customer hasn't paid in 30 days, send out a past due notice or call the customer to find out about the delay.

When you sell a product (or service), you receive cash and make a sale.

CUSTOMER	INVOICE NO.	DATE	AMOUNT	DUE DATE	PAID
ABC COMPANY	4322200	05-20-20	$1,200	06-20-20	
JONES, INC.	4322201	05-26-20	$2,000	06-26-20	

Table 23. Accounts receivable journal entries

BALANCE SHEET AS OF MARCH 31, 2020		CHANGE	NEW BALANCE
CASH IN CHECKING	$5,600	(A) $10.70 (B) -$0.70	$5,610.70 $2,610.00
ACCOUNTS RECEIVABLE	$25,000	(C) $10,000	$35,000.00
INVENTORY	$14,500	(D) -$7,000	$7,500.00
PREPAID INSURANCE & TAXES	$4,300		
UNEARNED REVENUE	$800		
PLANT ASSETS	$224,800		
LESS ACCUM DEPRECIATION	$-20,000		
TOTAL ASSETS	$255,000		
ACCOUNTS PAYABLE	$2,800		
SALES TAX PAYABLE	$1,200	(A) $0.70 (B) -$0.70	$1,200.70 $1,200.00
PAYROLL TAXES PAYABLE	$6,000		
CREDIT CARD PAYABLE	$1,500		
LOAN PAYABLE	$5,000		
NOTE PAYABLE OWNER	$205,000		
TOTAL LIABILITIES	$222,300		
COMMON STOCK	$500		
PREFERRED STOCK	$2,200		
RETAINED EARNINGS	$60,000		
DIVIDENDS	$-30,000		
TOTAL EQUITY	$32,700		
TOTAL LIABILITIES & EQUITY	$255,000		
INCOME STATEMENT MONTH ENDED MARCH 31, 2020			
SALES	$300,000	(A) 10.00 (C) $10,000	$300,010.00 $310,010.00
SALES RETURNS	$-15,000		
INTEREST INCOME	$100		
TOTAL REVENUE	$285,100		
COST OF GOODS SOLD	$148,500	(D) $7,000	$155,500.00
GROSS MARGIN	$136,600		
ADVERTISING EXPENSE	$6,500		
RENT EXPENSE	$3,800		
FEDERAL INCOME TAX	$600		
INSURANCE EXPENSE	$3,500		
UTILITIES EXPENSE	$6,000		
DUES & SUBSCRIPTIONS	$2,000		
GROSS WAGES	$78,000		
PAYROLL TAXES AND BENEFITS	$13,155		
INTEREST EXPENSE	$6,000		
BAD DEBT EXPENSE	$2,000		
DEPRECIATION EXPENSE	$6,000		
TOTAL EXPENSES	$127,555		
PROFIT/LOSS	$9,045		

SELLING

Remember Sally and her birdhouses? She sold her birdhouses for $10.00 each, plus sales tax of $0.70, for a grand total of $10.70.

Here's the journal entry for the sale:

CASH	$10.70
SALES	$10.00
SALES TAX PAYABLE	$0.70

Record sale of a birdhouse, and accompanying sales tax. See note **(A)**.

The sales tax amount is recorded as a liability (payable) because she has collected the tax from the customer and then has to pay it to her state tax department. At the end of the month, when she pays the tax, she would make another journal entry for the cash disbursement.

SALES TAX PAYABLE	$0.70
CASH	$0.70

Recording the payment of sales tax. See note **(B)**.

Let's assume a larger business has made a sale of $10,000 for an order of 100 widgets at $100 each, and the customer has 30 days to pay.

ACCOUNTS RECEIVABLE	$10,000
SALES	$10,000

Recording the sale of 100 widgets at $100 each. See note **(C)**.

The widgets cost the company $70 each to make.

COST OF GOODS SOLD	$7,000
INVENTORY	$7,000

Transferring the cost of manufacturing the widgets to COGS. See note **(D)**.

Notice that the widgets sold for $100 each and only cost $70 to build. The other $30 goes to cover overhead expenses, and hopefully leave a little for profit.

Sales and Cost of Goods Sold accounts appear on the Income Statement, as we've stated before. And Sales Tax Payable, Accounts Receivable, and Inventory accounts can be found on the balance sheet.

BALANCE SHEET AS OF MARCH 31, 2020		CHANGE	NEW BALANCE
CASH IN CHECKING	$5,600		
ACCOUNTS RECEIVABLE	$25,000	(A) -$500 (B) -$300	$24,500 $24,200
INVENTORY	$4,500		
PREPAID INSURANCE & TAXES	$4,300		
UNEARNED REVENUE	$800		
PLANT ASSETS	$234,800		
LESS ACCUM DEPRECIATION	$-20,000		
TOTAL ASSETS	$255,000		
ACCOUNTS PAYABLE	$2,800		
SALES TAX PAYABLE	$1,200		
PAYROLL TAXES PAYABLE	$6,000		
CREDIT CARD PAYABLE	$1,500		
LOAN PAYABLE	$5,000		
NOTE PAYABLE OWNER	$205,000		
TOTAL LIABILITIES	$222,300		
COMMON STOCK	$500		
PREFERRED STOCK	$2,200		
RETAINED EARNINGS	$60,000		
DIVIDENDS	$-30,000		
TOTAL EQUITY	$32,700		
TOTAL LIABILITIES & EQUITY	$255,000		
INCOME STATEMENT MONTH ENDED MARCH 31, 2020			
SALES	$300,000		
SALES RETURNS	$-15,000	(B) $-300	$-15,300
INTEREST INCOME	$100		
TOTAL REVENUE	$285,100		
COST OF GOODS SOLD	$148,500		
GROSS MARGIN	$136,600		
ADVERTISING EXPENSE	$6,500		
RENT EXPENSE	$3,800		
FEDERAL INCOME TAX	$600		
INSURANCE EXPENSE	$3,500		
UTILITIES EXPENSE	$6,000		
DUES & SUBSCRIPTIONS	$2,000		
GROSS WAGES	$78,000		
PAYROLL TAXES AND BENEFITS	$13,155		
INTEREST EXPENSE	$6,000		
BAD DEBT EXPENSE	$2,000	(A) $500	$2,500
DEPRECIATION EXPENSE	$6,000		
TOTAL EXPENSES	$127,555		
PROFIT/LOSS	$9,045		

In business there are cash sales and credit sales, as we've seen above. There are also bad debts, when a customer does not pay. You try to collect payment, you may even hire an attorney to try to collect for you, but the customer goes broke or just can't pay. So you have to write it off the books. You need to take the invoiced amount out of your accounts receivable, and post it to an expense account called "bad debt expense."

BAD DEBT EXPENSE	$500
ACCOUNTS RECEIVABLE	$500

To book a bad debt for customer invoice not paid. See note **(A)**.

Another situation that will come up when you sell products is returns. A customer may return some widgets because they were damaged or not what the customer expected. You will then give a credit for the damaged merchandise. Accountants use a revenue account called "sales returns and allowances," which is a contra account for sales, just like accumulated depreciation was a contra account for machinery in the earlier example.

SALES RETURNS AND ALLOWANCES	$300
ACCOUNTS RECEIVABLE	$300

To record the return of three widgets that were damaged. See note **(B)**.

The accounts Bad Debt Expense and Sales Returns can be found on the Income Statement. Accounts Receivable can be found on the Balance Sheet. See notes **(A)** and **(B)**.

BALANCE SHEET AS OF MARCH 31, 2020		CHANGE	NEW BALANCE
CASH IN CHECKING	$5,600		
ACCOUNTS RECEIVABLE	$25,000		
INVENTORY	$4,500		
PREPAID INSURANCE & TAXES	$4,300		
UNEARNED REVENUE	$800	(A) $40,000	$40,800
PLANT ASSETS	$234,800		
LESS ACCUM DEPRECIATION	$-20,000		
TOTAL ASSETS	$255,000		
ACCOUNTS PAYABLE	$2,800		
SALES TAX PAYABLE	$1,200		
PAYROLL TAXES PAYABLE	$6,000		
CREDIT CARD PAYABLE	$1,500		
LOAN PAYABLE	$5,000		
NOTE PAYABLE OWNER	$205,000		
TOTAL LIABILITIES	$222,300		
COMMON STOCK	$500		
PREFERRED STOCK	$2,200		
RETAINED EARNINGS	$60,000		
DIVIDENDS	$-30,000		
TOTAL EQUITY	$32,700		
TOTAL LIABILITIES & EQUITY	$255,000		
INCOME STATEMENT MONTH ENDED MARCH 31, 2020			
SALES	$300,000	(A) $40,000	$340,000
SALES RETURNS	$-15,000		
INTEREST INCOME	$100		
TOTAL REVENUE	$285,100		
COST OF GOODS SOLD	$148,500		
GROSS MARGIN	$136,600		
ADVERTISING EXPENSE	$6,500		
RENT EXPENSE	$3,800		
FEDERAL INCOME TAX	$600		
INSURANCE EXPENSE	$3,500		
UTILITIES EXPENSE	$6,000		
DUES & SUBSCRIPTIONS	$2,000		
GROSS WAGES	$78,000		
PAYROLL TAXES AND BENEFITS	$13,155		
INTEREST EXPENSE	$6,000		
BAD DEBT EXPENSE	$2,000		
DEPRECIATION EXPENSE	$6,000		
TOTAL EXPENSES	$127,555		
PROFIT/LOSS	$9,045		

RECEIVING ORDERS

When your business gets going, you will have more and more customers ordering product or services from you. The Big Town Company calls one day and orders 400 widgets for $100 each, and wants them delivered to their facility in two weeks. You agree to the terms, and you've made a sale.

UNEARNED REVENUE	$40,000
SALES	$40,000

Recording the order of 400 widgets at $100 each.

In this instance, we use the asset account called "unearned revenue" because we have not delivered the product, we've only received an order for it.

Unearned revenue is an asset account and will therefore show up on your Balance Sheet. See note **(A)**. It's an asset because you have a promise from a company to pay you that amount when you deliver the product. It's not accounts receivable until you deliver.

Since you have the order, you must now produce the goods.

BALANCE SHEET AS OF MARCH 31, 2020		CHANGE	NEW BALANCE
CASH IN CHECKING	$15,600	**(B)** -$7,000	$8,600
ACCOUNTS RECEIVABLE	$15,000		
INVENTORY	$4,500	**(A)** $18,000	$22,500
PREPAID INSURANCE & TAXES	$4,300		
UNEARNED REVENUE	$800		
PLANT ASSETS	$234,800		
LESS ACCUM DEPRECIATION	$-20,000		
TOTAL ASSETS	$255,000		
ACCOUNTS PAYABLE	$2,800	**(A)** $18,000	$20,800
SALES TAX PAYABLE	$1,200		
PAYROLL TAXES PAYABLE	$6,000	**(B)** $3,000	$9,000
CREDIT CARD PAYABLE	$1,500		
LOAN PAYABLE	$5,000		
NOTE PAYABLE OWNER	$205,000		
TOTAL LIABILITIES	$222,300		
COMMON STOCK	$500		
PREFERRED STOCK	$2,200		
RETAINED EARNINGS	$60,000		
DIVIDENDS	$-30,000		
TOTAL EQUITY	$32,700		
TOTAL LIABILITIES & EQUITY	$255,000		
INCOME STATEMENT MONTH ENDED MARCH 31, 2020			
SALES	$300,000		
SALES RETURNS	$-15,000		
INTEREST INCOME	$100		
TOTAL REVENUE	$285,100		
COST OF GOODS SOLD	$148,500		
GROSS MARGIN	$136,600		
ADVERTISING EXPENSE	$6,500		
RENT EXPENSE	$3,800		
FEDERAL INCOME TAX	$600		
INSURANCE EXPENSE	$3,500		
UTILITIES EXPENSE	$6,000		
DUES & SUBSCRIPTIONS	$2,000		
GROSS WAGES	$78,000	**(B)** $10,000	$88,000
PAYROLL TAXES AND BENEFITS	$13,155		
INTEREST EXPENSE	$6,000		
BAD DEBT EXPENSE	$2,000		
DEPRECIATION EXPENSE	$6,000		
TOTAL EXPENSES	$127,555		
PROFIT/LOSS	$9,045		

FULFILLING ORDERS

In order to produce the goods, you need materials and labor.

You buy the needed materials.

INVENTORY	$18,000
ACCOUNTS PAYABLE	$18,000

Recording purchase of materials to produce 400 widgets ordered, see note **(A)**.

Both of these accounts, Inventory and Accounts Payable, are on the Balance Sheet. See note **(A)**.

Then you pay employees to build the widgets. Of these wages, 80 percent (or $8,000) were direct labor, and 20 percent ($2,000) were administrative.

WAGES EXPENSE	$10,000
PAYROLL TAXES WITHHELD	$3,000
CASH	$7,000

Recording employees' wages paid, see note **(B)**.

BALANCE SHEET AS OF MARCH 31, 2020		CHANGE	NEW BALANCE
CASH IN CHECKING	$5,600		
ACCOUNTS RECEIVABLE	$25,000	(E) $40,000	$65,000
INVENTORY	$24,500	(D) -$18,000	$6,500
PREPAID INSURANCE & TAXES	$4,300		
UNEARNED REVENUE	$40,800	(E) -$40,000	$800
PLANT ASSETS	$174,800		
LESS ACCUM DEPRECIATION	$-20,000		
TOTAL ASSETS	$255,000		
ACCOUNTS PAYABLE	$2,800	(C) $2,000	$4,800
SALES TAX PAYABLE	$1,200		
PAYROLL TAXES PAYABLE	$6,000		
CREDIT CARD PAYABLE	$1,500		
LOAN PAYABLE	$5,000		
NOTE PAYABLE OWNER	$205,000		
TOTAL LIABILITIES	$222,300		
COMMON STOCK	$500		
PREFERRED STOCK	$2,200		
RETAINED EARNINGS	$60,000		
DIVIDENDS	$-30,000		
TOTAL EQUITY	$32,700		
TOTAL LIABILITIES & EQUITY	$255,000		
INCOME STATEMENT MONTH ENDED MARCH 31, 2020			
SALES	$300,000		
SALES RETURNS	$-15,000		
INTEREST INCOME	$100		
TOTAL REVENUE	$285,100		
COST OF GOODS SOLD	$148,500	(C) $2,000 (D) $26,000	$150,500 $176,500
GROSS MARGIN	$136,600		
ADVERTISING EXPENSE	$6,500		
RENT EXPENSE	$3,800		
FEDERAL INCOME TAX	$600		
INSURANCE EXPENSE	$3,500		
UTILITIES EXPENSE	$6,000		
DUES & SUBSCRIPTIONS	$2,000		
GROSS WAGES	$78,000	(D) -$8,000	$70,000
PAYROLL TAXES AND BENEFITS	$13,155		
INTEREST EXPENSE	$6,000		
BAD DEBT EXPENSE	$2,000		
DEPRECIATION EXPENSE	$6,000		
TOTAL EXPENSES	$127,555		
PROFIT/LOSS	$9,045		

You need to have another company process the products, something you can't do in your shop. This could be heat-treating metal products, painting, or some other finishing process.

SUBCONTRACT (COGS)	$2,000
ACCOUNTS PAYABLE	$2,000

Recording the cost of subcontracted finishing to widgets, see note **(C)**.

The Cost of Goods Sold account, as we saw earlier, can be found on the Income Statement. See note **(A)**.

The 400 widgets are now finished and ready to deliver. You move those costs to your cost of goods sold account to reflect the use of inventory items and labor for production.

COST OF GOODS SOLD	$26,000
INVENTORY	$18,000
WAGES EXPENSE	$8,000

Moving the direct costs of manufacturing 400 widgets to COGS, see note **(D)**.

When you deliver the products, you make this entry:

ACCOUNTS RECEIVABLE	$40,000
UNEARNED REVENUE	$40,000

Closing out unearned revenue and booking the receivable for 400 widgets delivered, see note **(E)**.

You take the sale out of unearned revenue because since it has been delivered, it is earned, and the customer now owes you payment in 30 days. So you prepare an invoice to be sent to the customer, and book the account receivable.

BALANCE SHEET AS OF MARCH 31, 2020		CHANGE	NEW BALANCE
CASH IN CHECKING	$5,600	(A) $40,000	$45,600
ACCOUNTS RECEIVABLE	$45,000	(A) -$40,000	$5,000
INVENTORY	$4,500		
PREPAID INSURANCE & TAXES	$4,300		
UNEARNED REVENUE	$800		
PLANT ASSETS	$214,800		
LESS ACCUM DEPRECIATION	$-20,000		
TOTAL ASSETS	$255,000		
ACCOUNTS PAYABLE	$2,800		
SALES TAX PAYABLE	$1,200		
PAYROLL TAXES PAYABLE	$6,000		
CREDIT CARD PAYABLE	$1,500		
LOAN PAYABLE	$5,000		
NOTE PAYABLE OWNER	$205,000		
TOTAL LIABILITIES	$222,300		
COMMON STOCK	$500		
PREFERRED STOCK	$2,200		
RETAINED EARNINGS	$60,000		
DIVIDENDS	$-30,000		
TOTAL EQUITY	$32,700		
TOTAL LIABILITIES & EQUITY	$255,000		
INCOME STATEMENT MONTH ENDED MARCH 31, 2020			
SALES	$300,000		
SALES RETURNS	$-15,000		
INTEREST INCOME	$100		
TOTAL REVENUE	$285,100		
COST OF GOODS SOLD	$148,500		
GROSS MARGIN	$136,600		
ADVERTISING EXPENSE	$6,500		
RENT EXPENSE	$3,800		
FEDERAL INCOME TAX	$600		
INSURANCE EXPENSE	$3,500		
UTILITIES EXPENSE	$6,000		
DUES & SUBSCRIPTIONS	$2,000		
GROSS WAGES	$78,000		
PAYROLL TAXES AND BENEFITS	$13,155		
INTEREST EXPENSE	$6,000		
BAD DEBT EXPENSE	$2,000		
DEPRECIATION EXPENSE	$6,000		
TOTAL EXPENSES	$127,555		
PROFIT/LOSS	$9,045		

RECEIVING PAYMENT

When the customer pays, you have a receipt of cash. Continuing with the above example for the order of 400 widgets, you would make this entry:

CASH	$40,000
ACCOUNTS RECEIVABLE	$40,000

Recording the payment by customer for the 400 widgets.

See note **(A)** on the Balance Sheet.

In order to stay on track, you should look at your invoices weekly and send out reminders to any past due customers.

When you finish a job, it's essential to determine if you've made a profit.

First, figure out your overhead costs. What does it cost you to do business? You're looking for indirect costs since direct costs were already accounted for. These indirect costs include:

- Rent for your shop or building
- Heat and electricity
- Phone and Internet
- Advertising
- Subscriptions and dues
- Travel expenses for business
- Administrative or management wages
- Employee benefits paid
- Insurance for the business
- Professional fees—accounting, IT, legal

Those are just some of the indirect costs of doing business. Calculate these costs for a month. Then figure out how many widgets you can make in a month (average). Then you can calculate an average overhead cost per widget (see table 24).

For your widget company, you pay rent of $1,500 per month, utilities of $500, phone and Internet of $250, advertising of $100, administrative wages of $500, benefits of $1,200, insurance of $300, and IT fees of $200. This totals $4,550 per month in indirect costs, or overhead.

Let's say your shop can produce 2,000 widgets per month. This means that the overhead cost per widget is $2.27.

OVERHEAD COSTS PER WIDGET	
RENT	$1,500
UTILITIES	$500
PHONE AND INTERNET	$250
ADVERTISING	$100
ADMINISTRATIVE WAGES	$500
BENEFITS	$1,200
INSURANCE	$300
IT FEES	$200
TOTAL OVERHEAD	$4,550 DIVIDED BY 2,000 WIDGETS = $2.275 OR $2.27

Table 24. Overhead costs per item

Say you sold 400 widgets for $40,000. It cost you $30,000 in direct costs to build them. And you paid out overhead of $908 for those widgets. So, you made a profit of $9,092 (see table 25).

Profit is the goal of any business, so you'll want to keep track of yours and the factors that affect it.

SALES	$40,000
COST OF GOODS SOLD	-30,000
GROSS MARGIN	$10,000
EXPENSES	$908
PROFIT	$ 9,092

Table 25. Calculating profit

5

////////////////////

END OF CYCLE

I n official accounting processes, at the end of each month, accountants perform a "month-end close," in which they reconcile balances and close out the revenue and expense accounts into the owner's equity account or the retained earnings account. Then all the revenue and expense accounts start fresh with a zero balance for the new month. After that, accountants typically prepare official financial statements for the month just closed and for year-to-date (of course, the statements can be prepared any time you need or want them).

In this chapter, we'll discuss some accounting items that you'll be closing out at regular intervals, as well as some new expenses that will crop up as your business starts to grow. Finally, we'll see how you can use all the information covered to assess the value of your business, or one that you might be considering for purchase.

BALANCE SHEET AS OF MARCH 31, 2020		CHANGE	NEW BALANCE
CASH IN CHECKING	$5,600	(A) -$2,500	$3,100.00
ACCOUNTS RECEIVABLE	$25,000		
INVENTORY	$4,500		
PREPAID INSURANCE & TAXES	$4,300	(A) $2,500 (B) -$208.33	$6,800.00 $6,591.67
UNEARNED REVENUE	$800		
PLANT ASSETS	$234,800		
LESS ACCUMULATED DEPRECIATION	$-20,000		
TOTAL ASSETS	$255,000		
ACCOUNTS PAYABLE	$2,800		
SALES TAX PAYABLE	$1,200		
PAYROLL TAXES PAYABLE	$6,000		
CREDIT CARD PAYABLE	$1,500		
LOAN PAYABLE	$5,000		
NOTE PAYABLE OWNER	$205,000		
TOTAL LIABILITIES	$222,300		
COMMON STOCK	$500		
PREFERRED STOCK	$2,200		
RETAINED EARNINGS	$60,000		
DIVIDENDS	$-30,000		
TOTAL EQUITY	$32,700		
TOTAL LIABILITIES & EQUITY	$255,000		
INCOME STATEMENT MONTH ENDED MARCH 31, 2020			
SALES	$300,000		
SALES RETURNS	$-15,000		
INTEREST INCOME	$100		
TOTAL REVENUE	$285,100		
COST OF GOODS SOLD	$148,500		
GROSS MARGIN	$136,600		
ADVERTISING EXPENSE	$6,500		
RENT EXPENSE	$3,800		
FEDERAL INCOME TAX	$600		
INSURANCE EXPENSE	$3,500	(B) $208.33	$3,708.33
UTILITIES EXPENSE	$6,000		
DUES & SUBSCRIPTIONS	$2,000		
GROSS WAGES	$78,000		
PAYROLL TAXES AND BENEFITS	$13,155		
INTEREST EXPENSE	$6,000		
BAD DEBT EXPENSE	$2,000		
DEPRECIATION EXPENSE	$6,000		
TOTAL EXPENSES	$127,555		
PROFIT/LOSS	$9,045		

INSURANCE

Every business should be insured. There are many different kinds of insurance coverage (general liability, premises, theft, etc.). You need to consult an insurance agent to discover which policies will best protect you and your business.

If you purchase an insurance policy, but only make a down payment, then you have a cash disbursement for that down payment. Each month, or quarter, when you make the next payment, you would post another cash disbursement (check) for that amount. This way you are expensing the insurance premium cost evenly throughout the year. Remember, one of the generally accepted accounting principles is the matching principle. Accountants try to closely match the timing of revenue and expenses.

If you pay the entire year's coverage up front, you would then have what is called a "prepaid expense." This is part of the accrual method of accounting. You would then post an asset called "prepaid insurance." Each month, you would take one month's premium value out of prepaid insurance and post it to insurance expense.

Let's say on January 1, you pay the insurance premium in full.

PREPAID INSURANCE	$2,500
CASH	$2,500

Recording the purchase of commercial insurance for the year. See note **(A)**.

On January 31, you would "book" one month of insurance used.

INSURANCE EXPENSE	$208.33
PREPAID INSURANCE	$208.33

Recording one month of insurance used. See note **(B)**.

With this journal entry, you now have "expensed" one month of insurance premium, and you have 11 months of insurance premium left to be used.

You would do that each month until December 31, when prepaid insurance would have a zero balance. This method ensures that the balance in the prepaid insurance account represents the value of insurance coverage that has been paid, but not "used." It's the value of future coverage, which is why it's an asset account (something you own).

The Prepaid Insurance and Taxes account can be seen on the Balance Sheet, and the Insurance Expense account can be seen on the Income Statement; see notes **(A)** and **(B)**.

BALANCE SHEET AS OF MARCH 31, 2020		CHANGE	NEW BALANCE
CASH IN CHECKING	$5,600		
ACCOUNTS RECEIVABLE	$25,000		
INVENTORY	$4,500		
PREPAID INSURANCE & TAXES	$4,300		
UNEARNED REVENUE	$800		
PLANT ASSETS	$234,800		
LESS ACCUM DEPRECIATION	$-20,000		
TOTAL ASSETS	$255,000		
ACCOUNTS PAYABLE	$2,800	(A) $2,400 (B) -$200	$5,200 $5,000
SALES TAX PAYABLE	$1,200		
PAYROLL TAXES PAYABLE	$6,000		
CREDIT CARD PAYABLE	$1,500		
LOAN PAYABLE	$5,000		
NOTE PAYABLE OWNER	$205,000		
TOTAL LIABILITIES	$222,300		
COMMON STOCK	$500		
PREFERRED STOCK	$2,200		
RETAINED EARNINGS	$60,000		
DIVIDENDS	$-30,000		
TOTAL EQUITY	$32,700		
TOTAL LIABILITIES & EQUITY	$255,000		
INCOME STATEMENT MONTH ENDED MARCH 31, 2020			
SALES	$300,000		
SALES RETURNS	$-15,000		
INTEREST INCOME	$100		
TOTAL REVENUE	$285,100		
COST OF GOODS SOLD	$148,500	(A) $2,400 (B) $-200	$150,900 $150,700
GROSS MARGIN	$136,600		
ADVERTISING EXPENSE	$6,500		
RENT EXPENSE	$3,800		
FEDERAL INCOME TAX	$600		
INSURANCE EXPENSE	$3,500		
UTILITIES EXPENSE	$6,000		
DUES & SUBSCRIPTIONS	$2,000		
GROSS WAGES	$78,000		
PAYROLL TAXES AND BENEFITS	$13,155		
INTEREST EXPENSE	$6,000		
BAD DEBT EXPENSE	$2,000		
DEPRECIATION EXPENSE	$6,000		
TOTAL EXPENSES	$127,555		
PROFIT/LOSS	$9,045		

PAYING SUPPLIERS

When you buy materials and supplies, you will probably be buying on credit. That means you'll be allowed to purchase the goods, then you will receive an invoice (bill), which you will have 30 days to pay.

When you do that, you incur an accounts payable, as discussed above.

Yet to be discussed are purchase orders. A purchase order (PO) is a form that you use to specify what you want to purchase and how much it's going to cost. You can also designate a job or project number for reference. Using purchase orders is a good way to prevent employee theft. Fill out one for every purchase, and use numbered forms so you'll know if a form is missing. Have an employee check every incoming shipment against purchase orders, so you'll know if something was ordered that you did not want or if you didn't get the product that you need for a job.

There are five steps to using purchase orders:

1. Fill out and submit a purchase order when you order materials or supplies, then file it.
2. When the materials/supplies are delivered, have a designated employee check it against the purchase order. If there is an issue with the order, deal with any discrepancies.
3. When everything checks out or is resolved, attach the PO to the invoice and file it with accounts payable.
4. If an order comes in without a PO, have your designated employee contact you. If there is no purchase order, it may be a fraudulent purchase.
5. Have a different employee receive the materials and check the purchase orders. This will decrease the likelihood of an employee ordering something for himself.

After the PO process is done and you've received your materials, you will receive the invoice, either included with the shipment or mailed to you. You will enter the invoice in your computer software as a bill that is due, also called an account payable.

MATERIALS	$2,400
ACCOUNTS PAYABLE	$2,400

Recording the receipt of supplies.

The materials account, a cost of goods sold account, is also called purchases by some companies. It can be seen on the Income Statement, note **(A)**.

As you go through your order, and compare it to the purchase order, you may find that you received a different part than what you ordered, or that some parts were broken or damaged. You call the supplier and make arrangements to have the items returned to them, and they give you a credit for the damaged or incorrect parts. You would then post the credit as purchases returns, which is a contra cost of goods sold account. That means it has a negative balance—or a balance opposite the purchases or materials account used above.

If you're using accounting software, you would enter a credit invoice, or a negative invoice, from that supplier. Then when you pay your bills, that amount would be subtracted from that supplier's other (previous) invoice that you were going to pay.

The journal entry would look like this:

ACCOUNTS PAYABLE	$200
PURCHASES RETURNS	$200

Recording the return of damaged parts for credit.

Materials and Purchases Returns will appear on the Income Statement in the Cost of Goods Sold section we saw above, note **(B)**.

MANAGING PAYROLL

In chapter 2 we discussed how to set up payroll; now we'll go through the payroll process and closeout. Each week, every other week, or every month you need to calculate your employees' gross wages, taxes and deductions, and net pay. Then you can write out their payroll checks.

If you want, you can break an employee's wage down by job or project to help you track costs. Calculating an employee's wages consists of the following steps:

1. Take an employee's hourly wage times the number of hours worked to calculate gross wages.
2. Take gross wages and multiply that by 1.45 percent (.0145) for Medicare tax and by 6.2 percent (.062) for Social Security tax.
3. Then, using the gross wages and the number of the employee's personal exemptions (from the employee's IRS Form W-4), find the applicable federal withholding tax from the IRS Federal Withholding Tax Tables, which can be found on the IRS website.

4. For state withholding taxes, use the applicable tax table found on the state's website, just as you used the federal tax table.

5. For local withholding taxes, take gross wages and multiply it by the applicable tax rate. This rate is found on the locality's website.

6. If there are any other deductions, such as child support or health insurance contributions, deduct them as well.

7. Subtract all the deductions from the gross wages to arrive at net pay. This is the amount you write the employee's check for.

At the end of the month, you need to summarize the wages and taxes withheld. You should maintain a payroll journal to keep running balances. Again, if you're using a computer accounting software package, this will be done for you behind the scenes, so you don't have to think about it. If you're using a manual system, just create a separate spreadsheet and list each paycheck—gross wages, taxes withheld, and net pay each in their own column—and keep totals for each month, quarter, and the year.

At the end of the year, you need to prepare W-2 Forms and provide these to your employees by January 31. They need to be filed with the Social Security Administration as well. These forms are available in office supply stores, and many accounting software packages will print them out for you within the system.

Table 26 shows what a payroll journal might look like for one quarter.

You would do that for each quarter, and then tally the totals for the year.

Your accounting software will automatically keep totals for all employees and their paychecks, so that every quarter and at the end of the year you will be able to easily determine each employee's wage and deductions. You will also be able to print out a W-2 Form. If you're keeping a manual set of books, you'll need to do this yourself.

PAYROLL JOURNAL						
DATE	GROSS WAGES	FEDERAL WITHHOLDING	SOCIAL SECURITY	STATE WITHHOLDING	LOCAL WITHHOLDING	NET PAY
JANUARY	$10,000	$1,400	$765	$235	$100	$7,500
FEBRUARY	$10,000	$1,400	$765	$235	$100	$7,500
MARCH	$10,000	$1,400	$765	$235	$100	$7,500

Table 26. Sample payroll journal detail

At the end of each pay period, when you issue paychecks, you may need to remit the federal withholding taxes right away (if your tax liability is $50,000 or greater in a six-month period), or you may only have to pay once a month.

To calculate your federal payroll tax liability, you will need to make a calculation. First, calculate the Social Security taxes withheld. Then multiply this amount by two. Why? Because the employee pays 7.65 percent of their wages for Social Security, and your company pays 7.65 percent to Social Security as well. Then add the federal withholding tax amount to the Social Security amount. This is the federal tax payment (called 941 tax) that you will pay to the IRS.

The total tax payment required, using the amounts shown in table 27, would be the total of $4,200 + $2,295 + $2,295 = $8,790.

These taxes should be paid online, at the IRS site for Electronic Federal Tax Payment System (EFTPS). The tax you are paying is referred to as 941 tax, since it is filed on IRS Form 941.

Table 27 provides an example.

Your state and local withholding taxes will usually be paid quarterly, unless your payroll is rather large. Tax forms can be found on the respective websites.

State unemployment taxes are paid quarterly, up to a certain wage limit set by your state. Again, you need to get the forms from the state department of taxation's website. You also need to register for all these taxes when you start your business.

Any workers' compensation insurance payments may be paid through a state program, or you may be able to self-insure. Find out from your state department of taxation.

FEDERAL PAYROLL TAXES DUE:	
FEDERAL WITHHOLDING TAXES WITHHELD	$4,200
SOCIAL SECURITY TAXES WITHHELD FROM THE EMPLOYEE	$2,295
SOCIAL SECURITY TAXES PAID BY THE EMPLOYER	$2,295
TOTAL TAX PAYMENT DUE	$8,790

Table 27. Federal payroll taxes liability, itemized and totaled

Federal unemployment taxes are calculated by taking employee wages (up to $7,000 each) times a percentage, available on the IRS website. At the point that your tax due reaches $500, you need to remit to the IRS. This tax, too, can be paid on the EFTPS website.

You should maintain a file for each employee, and keep their application forms, any performance reviews, wage increases, leaves, and so on documented in the file.

BALANCE SHEET AS OF MARCH 31, 2020		CHANGE	NEW BALANCE
CASH IN CHECKING	$5,600	(A) -$1,600 (B) -$400	$4,000 $3,600
ACCOUNTS RECEIVABLE	$25,000		
INVENTORY	$4,500		
PREPAID INSURANCE & TAXES	$4,300	(B) $400 (C) $1,200	$4,700 $3,500
UNEARNED REVENUE	$800		
PLANT ASSETS	$234,800		
LESS ACCUM DEPRECIATION	$-20,000		
TOTAL ASSETS	$255,000		
ACCOUNTS PAYABLE	$2,800		
SALES TAX PAYABLE	$1,200		
PAYROLL TAXES PAYABLE	$6,000		
CREDIT CARD PAYABLE	$1,500		
LOAN PAYABLE	$5,000		
NOTE PAYABLE OWNER	$205,000		
TOTAL LIABILITIES	$222,300		
COMMON STOCK	$500		
PREFERRED STOCK	$2,200		
RETAINED EARNINGS	$60,000		
DIVIDENDS	$-30,000		
TOTAL EQUITY	$32,700		
TOTAL LIABILITIES & EQUITY	$255,000		
INCOME STATEMENT MONTH ENDED MARCH 31, 2020			
SALES	$300,000		
SALES RETURNS	$-15,000		
INTEREST INCOME	$100		
TOTAL REVENUE	$285,100		
COST OF GOODS SOLD	$148,500		
GROSS MARGIN	$136,600		
ADVERTISING EXPENSE	$6,500		
RENT EXPENSE	$3,800		
FEDERAL INCOME TAX	$600	(A) $1,600 (C) $1,200	$2,200 $3,400
INSURANCE EXPENSE	$3,500		
UTILITIES EXPENSE	$6,000		
DUES & SUBSCRIPTIONS	$2,000		
GROSS WAGES	$78,000		
PAYROLL TAXES AND BENEFITS	$13,155		
INTEREST EXPENSE	$6,000		
BAD DEBT EXPENSE	$2,000		
DEPRECIATION EXPENSE	$6,000		
TOTAL EXPENSES	$127,555		
PROFIT/LOSS	$9,045		

PAYING INCOME TAXES

How you pay business income taxes depends on the legal structure of your business.

Federal Income Taxes

Sole proprietors (unincorporated businesses) pay income taxes personally, on their IRS Form 1040. So there is no business income tax.

Partners are in the same position as sole proprietors. They receive IRS Form K-1 from the business and use that to prepare their personal income tax returns. The business pays no tax—the partners do.

S corporation owners, just like partners, receive a Form K-1 and use that to file their personal income tax returns. Like sole proprietors and partners, they pay the tax personally. S corporations pay no federal tax.

Regular, or C corporations, do pay business income tax. Corporations file an IRS Form 1120, and they do pay income tax on their profits. Income taxes are calculated and paid with the tax return.

FEDERAL INCOME TAXES	$1,600
CASH	$1,600

Posting the payment of federal income taxes paid with return. See note **(A)**.

If a large amount is due, your tax preparer may set the business up to pay estimated tax payments throughout the year. You would post these to an asset account called prepaid taxes.

PREPAID TAXES	$400
CASH	$400

Recording payment of estimated federal taxes. See note **(B)**.

At the end of the year, when the real tax liability is calculated, you can move that amount to an expense account and leave the remainder, if any, in the account toward next year's tax liability.

FEDERAL INCOME TAX EXPENSE	$1,200
PREPAID TAXES	$1,200

Reclassifying federal income taxes paid on tax return. See note **(C)**.

State and local income taxes would be handled in the same manner.

Prepaid expenses are an Asset, and will appear on the Balance Sheet. Income Tax Expense will appear on the Income Statement. See the notes cited above.

BALANCE SHEET AS OF MARCH 31, 2020		CHANGE	NEW BALANCE
CASH IN CHECKING	$5,600	(A) -$2,000	$3,600
ACCOUNTS RECEIVABLE	$25,000		
INVENTORY	$4,500		
PREPAID INSURANCE & TAXES	$4,300		
UNEARNED REVENUE	$800		
PLANT ASSETS	$234,800		
LESS ACCUMULATED DEPRECIATION	$-20,000		
TOTAL ASSETS	$255,000		
ACCOUNTS PAYABLE	$2,800		
SALES TAX PAYABLE	$1,200		
PAYROLL TAXES PAYABLE	$6,000		
CREDIT CARD PAYABLE	$1,500		
LOAN PAYABLE	$5,000		
NOTE PAYABLE OWNER	$205,000		
TOTAL LIABILITIES	$222,300		
COMMON STOCK	$500		
PREFERRED STOCK	$2,200		
RETAINED EARNINGS	$60,000		
DIVIDENDS	$-30,000	(A) -$2,000	$-32,000
TOTAL EQUITY	**$32,700**		
TOTAL LIABILITIES & EQUITY	**$255,000**		
INCOME STATEMENT MONTH ENDED MARCH 31, 2020			
SALES	$300,000		
SALES RETURNS	$-15,000		
INTEREST INCOME	$100		
TOTAL REVENUE	$285,100		
COST OF GOODS SOLD	$148,500		
GROSS MARGIN	$136,600		
ADVERTISING EXPENSE	$6,500		
RENT EXPENSE	$3,800		
FEDERAL INCOME TAX	$600		
INSURANCE EXPENSE	$3,500		
UTILITIES EXPENSE	$6,000		
DUES & SUBSCRIPTIONS	$2,000		
GROSS WAGES	$78,000		
PAYROLL TAXES AND BENEFITS	$13,155		
INTEREST EXPENSE	$6,000		
BAD DEBT EXPENSE	$2,000		
DEPRECIATION EXPENSE	$6,000		
TOTAL EXPENSES	**$127,555**		
PROFIT/LOSS	**$9,045**		

PAYING DIVIDENDS

Corporations may pay dividends to its owners. Let's discuss retained earnings and corporate equity accounts.

Corporations don't have owner's equity accounts because presumably there are many owners. Stockholders (also called shareholders) may number just two or three, or they may number in the hundreds or thousands.

The corporate equity section on the balance sheet will have these accounts:

- Common stock
- Preferred stock
- Retained earnings
- Dividends paid
- Treasury stock

In an earlier chapter we discussed stocks; here let's discuss retained earnings.

This is a holding account for all the accumulated profits or losses of the corporation for as long as it's been in business. How does this happen? At the end of each year, when all the accounts have been summarized and reconciled, all your revenue and expense accounts are closed into retained earnings. This is called year-end close, which essentially closes out your year of business so you can start fresh in the new year with revenue and expenses. The balance sheet accounts of assets and liabilities are not part of this process.

Back when bookkeeping involved ledger books, the bookkeeper would make an entry to remove each account's balance and deposit the sum into the account retained earnings. Now accounting software packages do this automatically for you.

When a corporation pays dividends, it is returning a portion of those retained earnings to the stockholders. That is why the dividends account is another one of those contra accounts, with a balance opposite the balance of its "parent" account (retained earnings). So since Retained Earnings has a credit balance, Dividends will have a debit balance. On the Balance Sheet, Dividends has a minus sign by the balance.

Say a corporation pays a $200 dividend to its 10 stockholders. The journal entry would look like this:

DIVIDENDS	$2,000
CASH	$2,000

Recording the payment of dividends of $200 each to 10 stockholders.

The equity section of the Balance Sheet shows how an equity section for a corporation will look. See note **(A)**.

VALUING YOUR BUSINESS

At any time, you may want to know the value of your business. Of course, if you want to sell or liquidate it, you'll need to know the value. But even if neither of those is your intention, it is always a good idea to know your business's value.

A quick way to calculate that is to take a look at the equity section of your balance sheet. The balance sheet is an expression of the worth of your business itself, with assets representing the value of what you own, liabilities representing the amount of money you owe, and equity representing the balance of the two, which is the worth of your business.

In the simple balance sheet shown in table 28, you can see at a quick glance that the company's equity section shows a net worth (another name for owner's equity) of $7,000. That's the balance in the owner's equity section. But taking a closer look, you'll see that this company owns $9,250 in assets, $5,750 of cash, and $3,500 of accounts receivable. Cash is always worth its stated value, so there's no problem there. And accounts receivable should be easily collected if need be, so that value is good, too.

Next comes the liabilities section, or what this company owes. It owes a credit card bill of $950 and payroll taxes of $1,300. Since the cash and accounts receivable should be readily collected, there should be no problem paying these bills. So if this business owner needed to liquidate, he or she should have no problem turning the $9,250 in assets into cash, paying off the bills of $2,250, and having $7,000 left in hand.

When the company gets bigger, and has more noncurrent assets such as buildings, equipment, or investments, and more liabilities such as loans and notes, the situation gets a little more complicated. That's one reason depreciation is posted to the asset accounts—to more closely represent the actual value of the asset over time. With loans, the payoff value may be a bit different from the principal balance that is shown on the balance sheet. But the values should be approximate.

A potential buyer of a business should not look just at the equity section balance on the balance sheet, though. She should look at the assets and liabilities individually as well.

If an owner took a lot of money out of the business, it would cause the equity section on the balance sheet to look worse than it is, because doing so would decrease the balance in owner's equity (or retained earnings for a corporation). Remember, looking at owner's equity is a quick way to gauge the net worth of a business—it's the accumulation of profits for the business. But looking at the asset and liability values separately from the equity section would give a better indication of the business's value.

Another way of discerning the worth of a business is to take a denominator of 1.5 or 2 times the annual sales of the business. This is sometimes used for value approximation when selling a service business. The business may not have much in the way of actual in-hand assets, but it has value in its customer base and in its ability to make money.

The buyer should review at least three years of financial statements. Any accounting software can run a comparative financial statement that combines the last three years into one aggregate report. A business can have a really good year after a few bad ones, so reviewing three years of statements—as well as the average of at least three years of sales—is prudent.

Compare the balances. Compare the changes. Look at cash, expenses, costs—everything you've learned in this book. Really looking at the figures and comparing them from year to year is a great way to ascertain the value of the business.

Ultimately, your goal is to have a successful, thriving business. Whether you end up buying one, selling your own, or keeping and growing the one you started depends on your dreams and goals. Now that you have these accounting tools, you should be on the road to a successful business.

XYZ CLEANERS BALANCE SHEET AS OF JULY 31 2020		
ASSETS:		
CHECKING ACCOUNT	$5,750	
ACCOUNTS RECEIVABLE	$3,500	
TOTAL ASSETS		$9,250
LIABILITIES:		
CREDIT CARD PAYABLE	$950	
PAYROLL TAXES PAYABLE	$1,300	
TOTAL LIABILITIES	$2,250	
EQUITY:		
OWNER'S EQUITY	$7,000	
TOTAL LIAB. & EQUITY		$9,250

Table 28. Using the balance sheet for company valuation

INDEX

Made in the USA
Columbia, SC
18 September 2018